P9-ARV-507

test-prep your
IQ

By Alfred W. Munzert, Ph.D
Revised by Kim Munzert

THOMSON
ARCO

Australia • Canada • Mexico • Singapore • Spain • United Kingdom • United States

An ARCO Book
ARCO is a registered trademark of Thomson Learning, Inc., and is used herein under license by Peterson's.

About The Thomson Corporation and Peterson's
With revenues of US$7.8 billion, The Thomson Corporation (www.thomson.com) is a leading global provider of integrated information solutions for business, education, and professional customers. Its Learning businesses and brands (www.thomsonlearning.com) serve the needs of individuals, learning institutions, and corporations with products and services for both traditional and distributed learning.

Peterson's, part of The Thomson Corporation, is one of the nation's most respected providers of lifelong learning online resources, software, reference guides, and books. The Education Supersite[SM] at www.petersons.com—the Internet's most heavily traveled education resource—has searchable databases and interactive tools for contacting U.S.-accredited institutions and programs. In addition, Peterson's serves more than 105 million education consumers annually.

For more information, contact Peterson's, 2000 Lenox Drive, Lawrenceville, NJ 08648; 800-338-3282; or find us on the World Wide Web at: www.petersons.com/about

ISBN: 0-7689-1187-7

Printed in Canada
10 9 8 7 6 5 4 3 2 1 04 03 02

Acknowledgments

I would like to acknowledge the invaluable contribution of Mary Colvin, whose many hours of research and professional assistance have helped to make this book possible.

Alfred W. Munzert, Ph.D.

I would like to acknowledge my father, the late Alfred W. Munzert, who taught and gave me far more than I could ever imagine.

Kim Munzert

Contents

Introduction

Test-Prep Your IQ has been written with two goals in mind:

The first, and the most important, goal of this book is to help you understand your strengths and weaknesses so that you can score high on standardized IQ tests. Our proven test-taking strategies will not only help you feel more confident about taking standardized tests but will also improve your performance. The IQ test in this book will help you practice your test-taking skills and help you learn more about yourself and your strengths.

The second goal of this book is to have some fun. So, dive in!

Why You Need This Book

Like it or not, multiple-choice tests play a pretty large role in people's lives today—more so than ever before. In truth, high school teachers and college professors are actually *in love* with multiple-choice tests. Think of those pesky Advanced Placement tests and college entrance exams like the SAT and ACT Assessment that all use multiple-choice questions. Bottom line: You can't escape multiple-choice tests, so you might as well have fun while you learn to master them. The test in this book is not like most multiple-choice tests, but it *is* multiple choice and it *will* exercise your brain!

About IQ Tests

Underlying the desire to find our IQ (Intelligence Quotient) is the question, "Will I be successful?" An IQ test alone cannot completely answer or determine this. It may, however, aid in our appraisal of ourselves. It can surely add insight into our logical thinking and academic abilities and talents. This book attempts not only to shed light on attributes of your IQ but also to enlighten you to talents and assets that you may not have considered to be important or even a part of your intelligence. In addition to the IQ test, there are many topics to explore within this book, including:

- Strategies for Taking Multiple-Choice Tests
- The Role of the Left Brain and Right Brain in Logic and Creativity
- Can Your IQ Be Improved or Impaired?
- Improving Your Ability to Learn and Think
- Creativity, Leadership, and Motor Skills As Forms of Intelligence
- Find Out if You Are Exceptionally Gifted
- Exercising the Brain
- Computers and Intelligence

Enjoy this book and use it to learn about yourself and your talents.

Test-Taking Strategies

The Multiple-Choice Test

The test in this book is an IQ test. In this section, we'll give you some general multiple-choice test-taking tips to help you succeed with multiple-choice tests.

Many people think that a multiple-choice test simply requires the test-taker to use recognition skills to pick out or recognize facts. Unfortunately, that isn't true—sorry! A multiple-choice test can be simple or very difficult. It can measure recognition skills or it can measure higher order thinking skills such as *application*, *comprehension*, *analysis*, or *synthesis*. A well-written multiple-choice test will most likely contain questions that range from simple to difficult and will measure a number of different levels of thinking. So, to be a successful test-taker, you've got to know about the different kinds of multiple-choice questions and the best strategies for answering them. Let's begin with the questions, and then we'll talk briefly about some strategies to help you ace that exam!

A multiple-choice question has two elements:

1. The stem (or question)
2. The answer choices

The stem may be in the form of a question:

EXAMPLE: What painter is considered the "father of modern art"?

Or, the stem may be in the form of an incomplete statement:

EXAMPLE: The "father of modern art" is

In the first case, the correct answer will answer the question that is asked. In the second example, the answer will accurately complete the incomplete statement. For both questions, the answer would be the same: Cezanne. Occasionally, however, multiple-choice stems will contain words such as *except* or *not:*

> **EXAMPLE:** All of the following are associated with ballet *except*
>
> **EXAMPLE:** Which of the following is *not* associated with ballet?

In cases such as these, the multiple-choice question is essentially a true/false question. The correct answer choice is the one that is *not* true or is the exception to the statement. For example, if "John Bon Jovi" was given as an answer choice for either question above, you should choose it because John Bon Jovi is a rock star—and is *not* associated with ballet. This may seem overly simple, but these kinds of questions often confuse test-takers. Strategies regarding these questions will be addressed later in the chapter.

Answer choices probably won't vary much from test to test with regard to format, but there might be one or two small exceptions. First, the questions will usually have either four or five answer choices. Tests in high school or college often will vary and may have either fewer than four or more than five answer choices, depending on the personality of the instructor, the level of difficulty of the test, and the material that is being tested. However, most standardized tests will use either four or five answer choices. The second way tests might differ is how the answers are listed. Some exams will use lettered answer choices (A, B, C, D, and E), while others will use numbered choices (1, 2, 3, 4, and 5). Regardless of how the answers are listed, the strategies for answering the questions remain the same.

Strategies for Answering Multiple-Choice Questions

Unfortunately, there is no one strategy that will enable you to correctly answer *every* question on *every* test you take. And there is no substitute for a solid, working knowledge of the subject matter being tested. In other words, test-taking strategies are going to be most effective when you combine them with good study habits. So, if you're looking for a shortcut that relieves you of actually studying the material being tested, you've come to the wrong place. (And if you ever find that place where no studying is necessary, let us know; we'd love to go there!) That being said, let's look at some of the most effective strategies for taking multiple-choice tests.

1. **Read the question carefully.** This suggestion seems really obvious, but it is probably the *most important* and the most overlooked strategy. Realizing you answered a question incorrectly because you didn't read it carefully is pretty frustrating. So, read the question carefully, and make sure you know exactly what the question is asking. As you read the question, look for any key words within the stem that have significance. You may also find it helpful to circle the key words in the stem when you see them. This will reinforce the key words in your mind. For example, if the question includes a negative, circle the negative and treat the question as a true/false question. As mentioned earlier, some multiple-choice questions contain negatives like *except* or *not*. When you encounter a negative, circle it, underline it, or put a star by it. First, this will help you remember that there is a negative in the question. Second, this will help you remember that you are looking for a false statement in the answer choices.

   EXAMPLE:

   All of the following are types of paint *except*

   (A) tempera.

   (B) charcoal.

   (C) oil.

   (D) acrylic.

   (E) watercolor.

When answering this question, make sure you circle the word *except* so you remember that you are looking for the answer that does not make the stem true. If you were to choose answer choice (B), you would be correct.

2. **Read every answer choice carefully before you make your selection.** This is another suggestion that may seem obvious, but it is of the utmost importance. Read every answer choice, even if you think you know the answer. In other words, although you think you know the answer is (B), and (B) may be a *good* answer, (D) may be the *best* answer to the question.

3. **Use the process of elimination.** If you read all of the answer choices, and you still don't know the correct answer right away, use the process of elimination to narrow your choices. Usually, multiple-choice questions will have a set of answer choices that includes a very unlikely answer, one or two poor answers, a possible answer, and a best answer. You should read through the answer choices and cross out any that you are sure are incorrect. The more you can narrow down the choices, the better your odds if you have to guess. Most of the time, you will be able to narrow the choices to two or three possible answers. With these odds (1:2 or 1:3), guessing will usually produce a higher score than if you leave the question unanswered.

EXAMPLE:

Of the following, who is a writer?

(A) Chewbacca the Wookie

(B) Kermit the Frog

(C) Ghengis Khan

(D) The Old Woman Who Lived in a Shoe

(E) Dave Barry

The correct answer is (E). Even if you've never heard of Dave Barry, we're hoping you were able to figure out that the other choices definitely are *not* writers!

4. **Take the question at face value.** Take each question at face value and don't try to read too much into it. Don't try to "read between the lines" or overanalyze what the question is asking. By overanalyzing, you run the risk of misinterpreting the question, thereby seriously decreasing your chances of choosing the correct answer. There are such things as trick questions. You can find them on all sorts of tests. You want to be on the lookout, but don't obsess by looking for a trick question around every corner.

5. **Look for absolutes within the answer choices.** As you read through all the answer choices, watch for absolutes such as *all*, *never*, *none*, and *always*. These are absolutes because these words leave no room for exceptions of any kind. Unless you specifically remember a major point of emphasis on whatever the subject of the question is, the answer choice or choices containing an absolute are probably not correct:

EXAMPLE:

Which of the following can be said of American colonists under British rule?

(A) All colonists wanted to be free of British rule.

(B) All colonists wanted to drink tea.

(C) Colonists were never forced to board British soldiers.

(D) Colonists who were unhappy with British rule organized to fight for freedom.

(E) Colonists were always very unhappy with British rule.

If you read the answer choices carefully, you probably noticed that choices (A), (B), (C) and (E) contain absolutes. Therefore, you can be fairly certain that these are incorrect. You probably already knew that (D) is the correct answer, but in case you didn't, you could have figured it out with the strategy in the paragraph above.

6. **Don't spend too much time on any one question.** Practically all standardized tests have a time limit. This means that you, as the test-taker, must manage your time wisely. It isn't uncommon for a test to require an average of less than one minute per answer. Therefore, if you encounter a question that really stumps you, put a star next to it and move on. If you have time to work on it after you answer all the other questions, go back to it. It is much more productive to spend your time answering other questions than spending precious time struggling with one. On this IQ test, you can guess as we don't penalize you for wrong answers.

   EXAMPLE:

   What was the first race horse to win $1 million in his career?

   (A) Man O'War

   (B) Secretariat

   (C) Citation

   (D) Cigar

   (E) Gallant Fox

   Do you know the answer to this question? If so, kudos to you. If not, do you really think you'll figure it out by just staring at the answer choices? Probably not. Therefore, why spend precious time racking your brain on this question when you could be answering other questions?

7. **Don't change your answers.** The oldest test-taking strategy in the history of test-taking strategies is "go with your first choice." If you choose an answer and then feel an urge to change the answer later, the urge is probably just nerves. Don't second-guess yourself. There was probably a reason you chose the answer you did. Therefore, don't change an answer unless you are positively sure that the answer you chose is incorrect *and* you are absolutely sure you know which answer is correct.

Good Luck!

part 1

The Self-Scoring IQ Test

About This Exam

On the following pages, you will take a carefully constructed test designed to measure your intelligence. This test was designed for anyone 11 years old or older. Take the test only when you are in a fresh state of mind and in a quiet, comfortable work area with good lighting. Please observe the time restrictions, and do not discuss the questions with anyone else while taking the test.

A scoring table follows the test. Explanations of the answers will help you understand the basis of the test.

Sample Questions

Carefully study the following sample questions before beginning the test.

1. In some questions, you will be asked to make a comparison.

   EXAMPLE: Which one of the five makes the best comparison?

   Boat is to water as airplane is to:

SUN	GROUND	WATER	SKY	TREE
(A)	(B)	(C)	(D)	(E)

   The correct answer is (D). A boat travels through water. This can be compared to an airplane that travels through the sky.

You also will be asked to compare designs.

EXAMPLE: Which one of the five makes the best comparison?

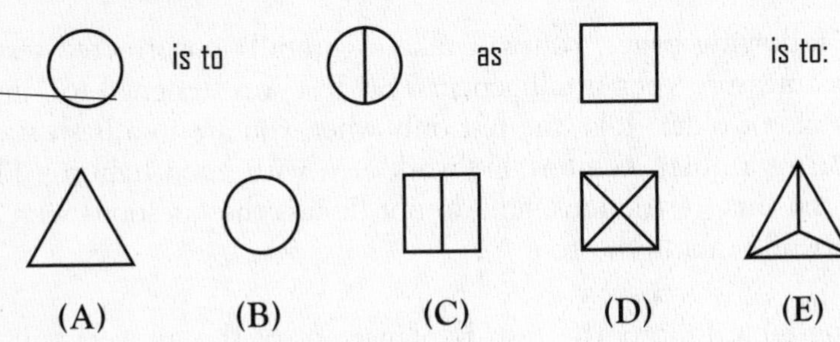

The correct answer is (C). A circle that is divided into two parts can be compared to a square that is also divided into two parts.

2. In some questions, you will be given a group of five things. Four of them will have something in common; they will be similar in some way. You will be asked to choose the one that is not similar to the others.

EXAMPLE: Which one of the five is least like the other four?

DOG	CAR	CAT	BIRD	FISH
(A)	(B)	(C)	(D)	(E)

The correct answer is (B). The others are all living creatures. A car is not alive.

These questions may also be based on designs.

EXAMPLE: Which one of the five is least like the other four?

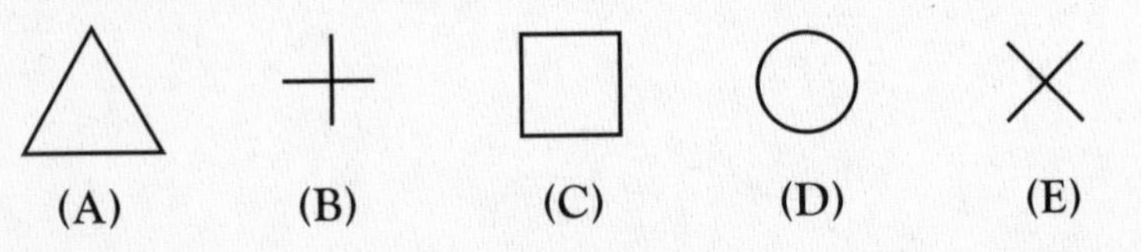

(A) (B) (C) (D) (E)

The correct answer is (D). The others are all made with straight lines. A circle is a curved line.

3. In some questions, you will be given numbers or letters that are in a certain order. They follow some pattern of arrangement. However, one of them will not fit. You will be asked to choose the one that does not fit into the pattern.

   EXAMPLE: Which one of the numbers does not belong in the following series?

   1 3 5 7 9 10 11 13

   The correct answer is 10. Starting with 1, the odd numbers are arranged in order; 10 is an even number, which does not fit in the series.

4. There will be some problems that you will be asked to solve. These will not require any difficult math. Instead, they will be testing how logical you are—that is, how well you think.

You are now ready to begin the test. Read each question carefully and write the letter of your answer or the number that you choose in the space next to the question number on the answer sheet on page 15. Tear out the answer sheet before you begin.

Instructions

1. You have 45 minutes to answer the 60 questions. Do not exceed this time limit.

2. Answer all questions. If you do not know the answer, guess. Guessing has been considered in the scoring. Do not leave any question unanswered.

3. If a question seems to have more than one answer or no correct answers at all, pick what you consider to be the best of the choices given. These questions are purposely designed to test your ability to think and reason.

Answer Sheet

Before you begin the IQ Test on page 17, tear out this page and place it beside your book.

Write the letter or number of your answer choice on the line beside the question number.

1. _____	16. _____	31. _____	46. _____
2. _____	17. _____	32. _____	47. _____
3. _____	18. _____	33. _____	48. _____
4. _____	19. _____	34. _____	49. _____
5. _____	20. _____	35. _____	50. _____
6. _____	21. _____	36. _____	51. _____
7. _____	22. _____	37. _____	52. _____
8. _____	23. _____	38. _____	53. _____
9. _____	24. _____	39. _____	54. _____
10. _____	25. _____	40. _____	55. _____
11. _____	26. _____	41. _____	56. _____
12. _____	27. _____	42. _____	57. _____
13. _____	28. _____	43. _____	58. _____
14. _____	29. _____	44. _____	59. _____
15. _____	30. _____	45. _____	60. _____

IQ Test

1. Which of the five makes the best comparison?

YYZZZYZZY is to 221112112 as YYZZYZZY is to:

221221122	22112122	22112112	112212211	212211212
(A)	(B)	(C)	(D)	(E)

2. Which of the five is least like the other four?

NICKEL	TIN	STEEL	IRON	COPPER
(A)	(B)	(C)	(D)	(E)

3. Which of the five designs makes the best comparison?

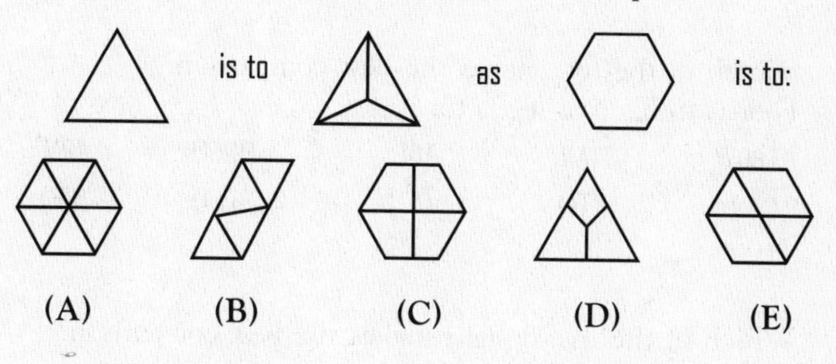

4. Which of the five designs is least like the other four?

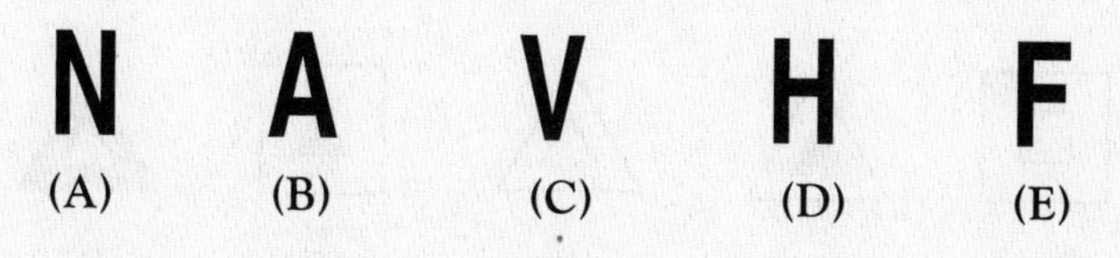

5. Jerry received both the fifteenth highest and the fifteenth lowest mark in the class. How many students are in the class?

15	25	29	30	32
(A)	(B)	(C)	(D)	(E)

6. Which of the five is least like the other four?

DICTIONARY	BIOGRAPHY	ATLAS	ALMANAC	DIRECTORY
(A)	(B)	(C)	(D)	(E)

7. Which of the five is least like the other four?

A	Z	F	N	H
(A)	(B)	(C)	(D)	(E)

8. Which of the five makes the best comparison?
Foot is to hand as leg is to:

ELBOW	PIANO	TOE	FINGER	ARM
(A)	(B)	(C)	(D)	(E)

9. Which of the five designs makes the best comparison?

 is to  as  is to:

(A) (B) (C) (D) (E)

10. If all Ferpies are Worgs and no Worgs are Sprickles, then no Sprickles are definitely Ferpies.
This statement is definitely:

TRUE	FALSE	NEITHER
(A)	(B)	(C)

11. Of the following numbers, which one is least like the others?

1 3 5 7 11 13 15 17 19

12. Which of the five designs is least like the other four?

D	G	C	P	R
(A)	(B)	(C)	(D)	(E)

13. Terry is older than Mark, and Sam is younger than Terry. Which of the following statements is most accurate?

(A) Sam is older than Mark.
(B) Sam is younger than Mark.
(C) Sam is as old as Mark.
(D) It is impossible to tell whether Sam or Mark is older.

14. Which of the five designs is least like the other four?

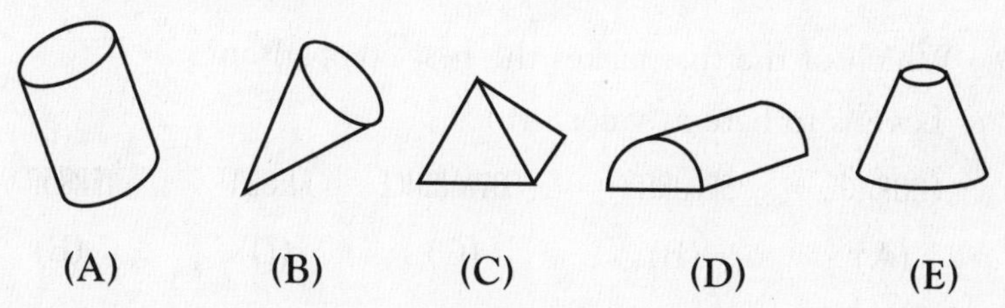

(A) (B) (C) (D) (E)

15. Which of the five makes the best comparison?

Leap is to peal as 8326 is to:

2368	6283	2683	6328	3628
(A)	(B)	(C)	(D)	(E)

16. Anne received $0.59 in change from a supermarket purchase. Of the eleven coins she received in change, three were exactly alike. These three coins had to be:

PENNIES	NICKELS	DIMES	QUARTERS	HALF DOLLARS
(A)	(B)	(C)	(D)	(E)

17. Which of the five is least like the other four?

PECK	OUNCE	PINT	CUP	QUART
(A)	(B)	(C)	(D)	(E)

18. Three enemy messages were intercepted at communications headquarters. The code was broken, and it was found that "Berok tenlis krux" means "Secret attack Wednesday," "Baroom zax tenlis" means "Secret plans included," and "Gradnor berok plil elan" means "Wednesday victory is ours." What does "krux" mean?

SECRET	WEDNESDAY	NOTHING	ATTACK	PLANS
(A)	(B)	(C)	(D)	(E)

19. Which of the five makes the best comparison?

Love is to hate as valor is to:

COURAGE	SECURITY	COWARDICE	ANGER	TERROR
(A)	(B)	(C)	(D)	(E)

20. The price of an article was cut 50% for a sale. By what percent must the price of the item be increased to again sell the item at the original price?

25%	50%	75%	100%	200%
(A)	(B)	(C)	(D)	(E)

21. Which of the five designs makes the best comparison?

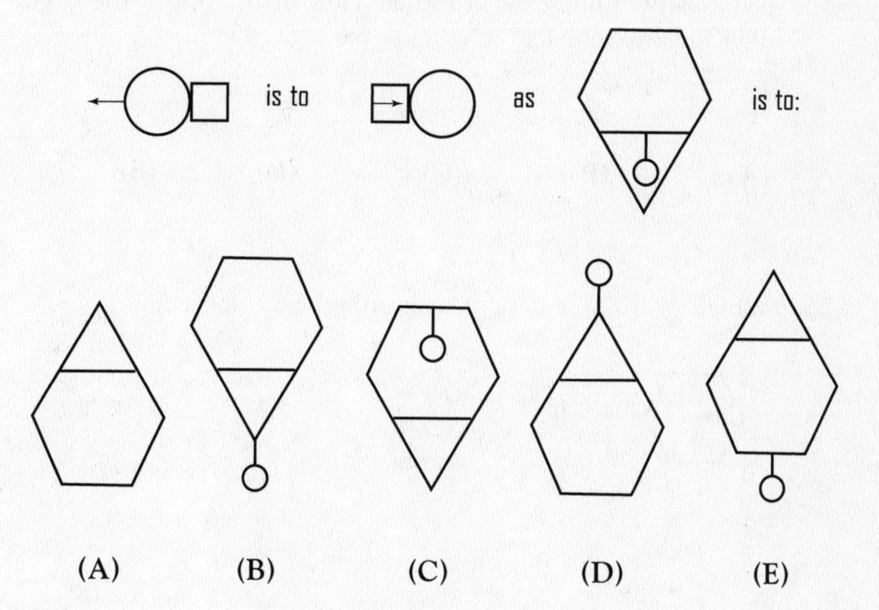

22. Which of the five is least like the other four?

SQUASH	PUMPKIN	TOMATO	CUCUMBER	CORN
(A)	(B)	(C)	(D)	(E)

23. Which of the five makes the best comparison?

Hole is to donut as pages are to:

STORY	WORDS	CONTENTS	INDEX	COVER
(A)	(B)	(C)	(D)	(E)

24. Kim was sent to the store to get 11 large cans of fruit. Kim could carry only 2 cans at a time. How many trips to the store did Kim have to make?

5	$5\frac{1}{2}$	6	$6\frac{1}{2}$	7
(A)	(B)	(C)	(D)	(E)

25. Which of the five designs makes the best comparison?

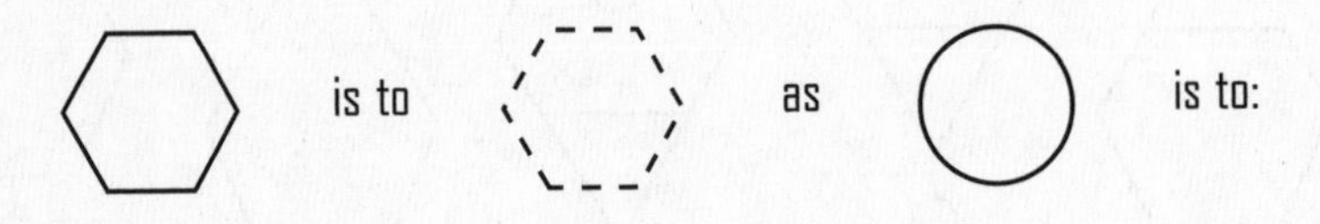

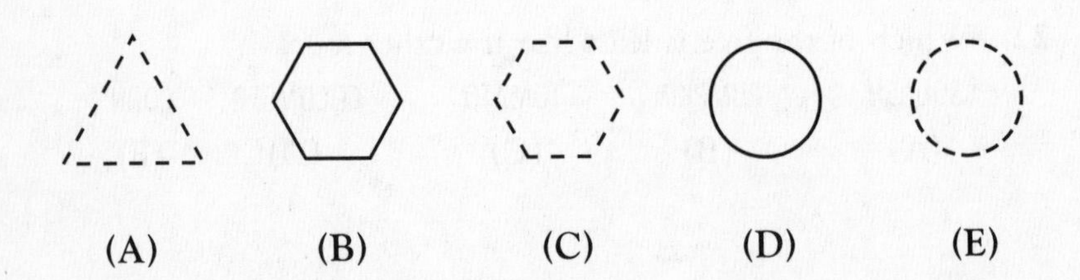

(A) (B) (C) (D) (E)

26. If all Pleeps are Floops and all Floops are Leepies, then all Pleeps are definitely Leepies.
This statement is definitely:

TRUE	FALSE	NEITHER
(A)	(B)	(C)

27. Which of the five designs is least like the other four?

X	T	N	V	L
(A)	(B)	(C)	(D)	(E)

28. Jim, John, Jerry, and Joe together bought a basket of 144 apples. Jim received 10 more apples than John, 26 more than Jerry, and 32 more than Joe. How many apples did Jim receive?

73	63	53	43	27
(A)	(B)	(C)	(D)	(E)

29. Which of the five is least like the other four?

TOUCH	SEE	HEAR	EAT	SMELL
(A)	(B)	(C)	(D)	(E)

30. Which of the five makes the best comparison?
Daughter is to father as niece is to:

NEPHEW	COUSIN	UNCLE	MOTHER	BROTHER
(A)	(B)	(C)	(D)	(E)

31. Which of the five designs is least like the other four?

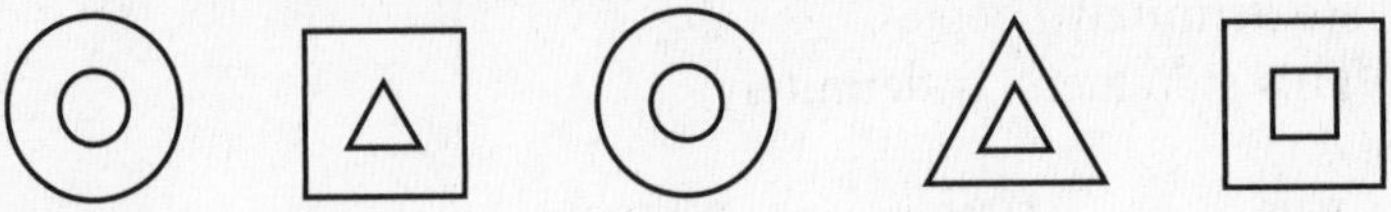

(A) (B) (C) (D) (E)

32. Which number does not belong in the following series?

4 5 8 10 11 16 19 32 36

33. Which of the five makes the best comparison?

Bark is to tree as scales are to:

GILLS	ELEPHANT	BUTCHER	FISH	SKIN
(A)	(B)	(C)	(D)	(E)

34. Which of the five is least like the other four?

TURKEY	DUCK	CHICKEN	PHEASANT	GOOSE
(A)	(B)	(C)	(D)	(E)

35. The secher vlooped quaply berak the kriggly lool. Then the secher _____ flaxly down the kleek.

Which word belongs in the space?

VLOOPED	QUAPLY	BERAK	LOOL	KRIGGLY
(A)	(B)	(C)	(D)	(E)

36. The fish has a head 9 inches long. The tail is equal to the size of the head plus one half the size of the body. The body is the size of the head plus the tail. How long is the fish?

27 inches	54 inches	63 inches	72 inches	81 inches
(A)	(B)	(C)	(D)	(E)

37. Which of the five designs is least like the other four?

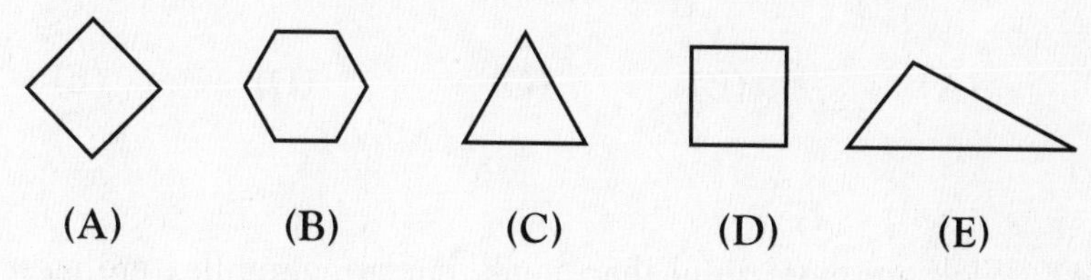

(A) (B) (C) (D) (E)

38. If you rearrange the letters in "NAICH," you would have the name of a(n):

COUNTRY	OCEAN	STATE	CITY	ANIMAL
(A)	(B)	(C)	(D)	(E)

39. Jack is 15 years old, three times as old as his sister. How old will Jack be when he is twice as old as his sister?

18	20	24	26	30
(A)	(B)	(C)	(D)	(E)

40. Which of the five designs makes the best comparison?

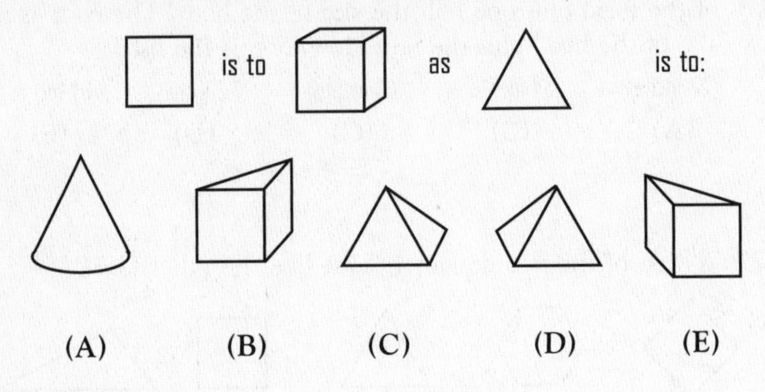

41. Slok are more zitful than mulk, but pringling flex are most _____ of all.

Which word belongs in the blank space?

SLOK	ZITFUL	MULK	PRINGLING	FLEX
(A)	(B)	(C)	(D)	(E)

42. Which of the five makes the best comparison?

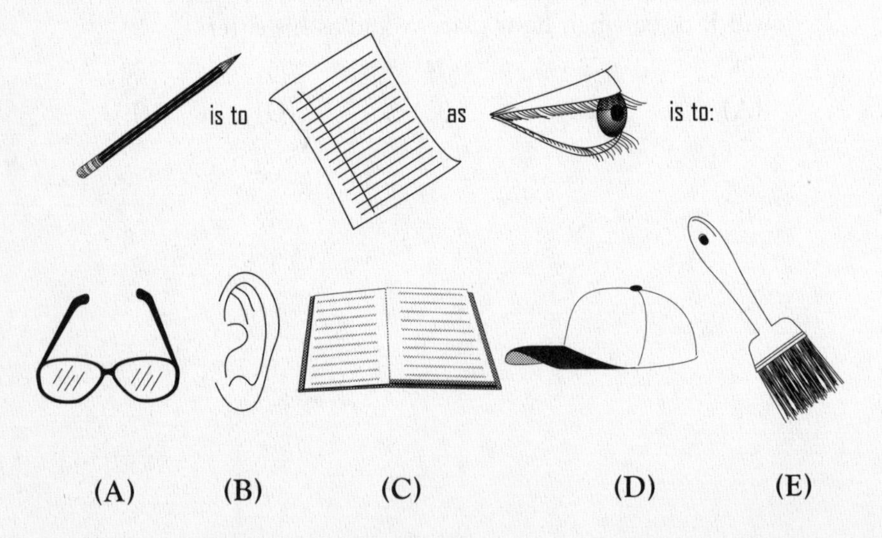

43. If you rearrange the letters in "SHORE," you would have the name of a(n):

COUNTRY	OCEAN	STATE	CITY	ANIMAL
(A)	(B)	(C)	(D)	(E)

44. Which number does not belong in the following series?

1 3 5 7 9 11 12 13 15

45. Which of the five makes the best comparison?

Gas is to car as food is to:

MOUTH	STOMACH	ENERGY	BODY	TEETH
(A)	(B)	(C)	(D)	(E)

46. Which of the five designs is least like the other four?

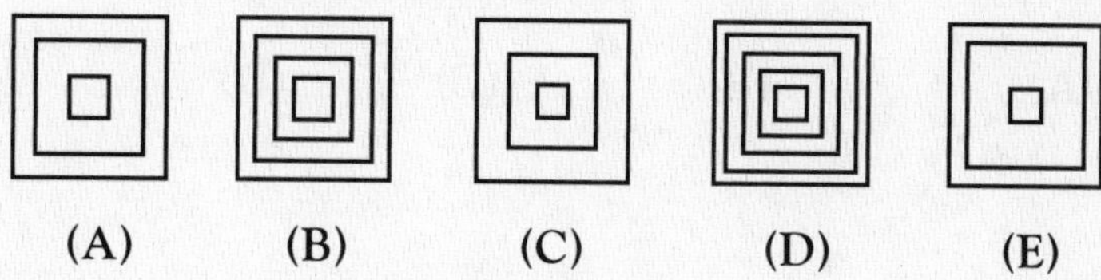

(A) (B) (C) (D) (E)

47. Which of the five is least like the other four?

WICHITA	DALLAS	CANTON	BANGOR	FRESNO
(A)	(B)	(C)	(D)	(E)

48. If some Tripples are Tropples and all Bolars are Tropples, then some Tripples are definitely Bolars.

This statement is:

TRUE	FALSE	NEITHER
(A)	(B)	(C)

49. Which of the five designs makes the best comparison?

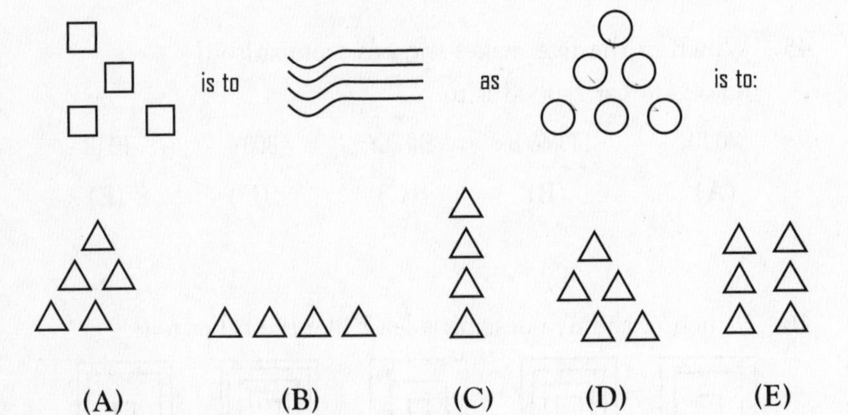

50. Which of the five makes the best comparison?

Light is to moon as book is to:

TACK	CHECK	TURF	BURN	TOY
(A)	(B)	(C)	(D)	(E)

51. Which of the five designs is least like the other four?

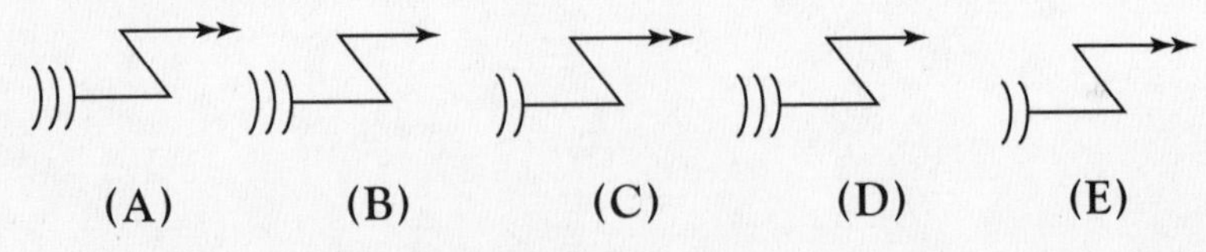

52. Which letter does not belong in the following series?

B E H K M N Q T

53. Which of the five makes the best comparison?

Pillow is to pillowcase as arm is to:

BODY	SLEEVE	HAND	GLOVE	RING
(A)	(B)	(C)	(D)	(E)

54. Which of the five is least like the other four?

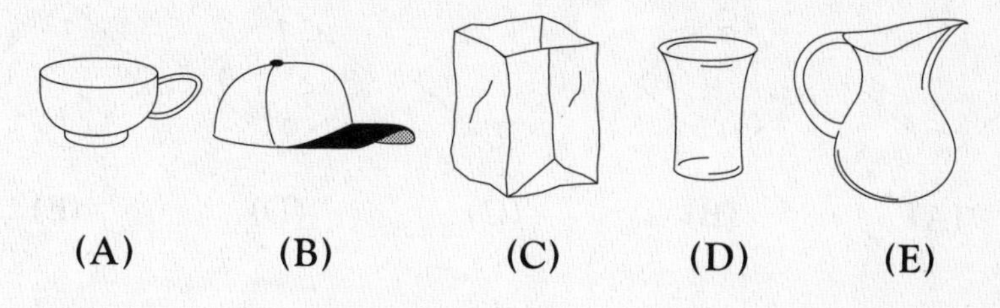

(A) (B) (C) (D) (E)

55. Which of the five is least like the other four?

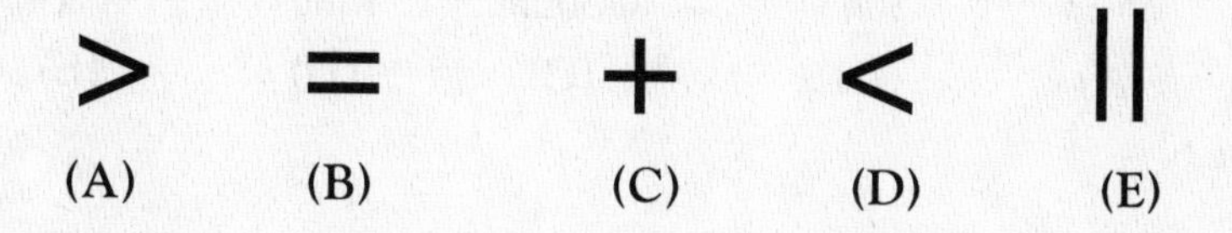

(A) (B) (C) (D) (E)

56. If all Truples are Glogs and some Glogs are Glips, then some Truples are definitely Glips.

This statement is:

TRUE	FALSE	NEITHER
(A)	(B)	(C)

57. If you rearrange the letters in "TALCATIN," you would have the name of a(n):

COUNTRY	OCEAN	STATE	CITY	ANIMAL
(A)	(B)	(C)	(D)	(E)

58. Which of the five is least like the other four?

ARTIST	GOLFER	NEWSCASTER	DANCER	MECHANIC
(A)	(B)	(C)	(D)	(E)

59. Which of the five does not belong in the series?

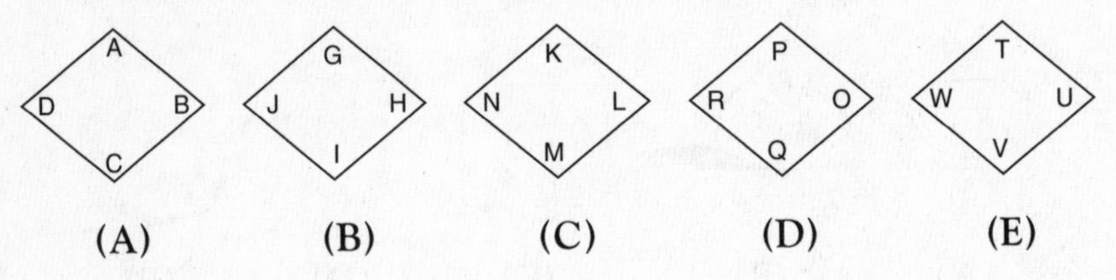

(A) (B) (C) (D) (E)

60. Which of the five is least like the other four?

WATER	SUN	GASOLINE	WIND	CEMENT
(A)	(B)	(C)	(D)	(E)

Answers and Explanations

1. Which of the five makes the best comparison?

   YYZZZYZZY is to 221112112 as YYZZYZZY is to:

221221122	22112122	22112112	112212211	212211212
(A)	(B)	(C)	(D)	(E)

The correct answer is (C). Substitute numbers for letters: Y = 2 and Z = 1.

2. Which of the five is least like the other four?

NICKEL	TIN	STEEL	IRON	COPPER
(A)	(B)	(C)	(D)	(E)

The correct answer is (C). (Steel) The others are simple metals; steel is an alloy (combination of two or more metals).

3. Which of the five designs makes the best comparison?

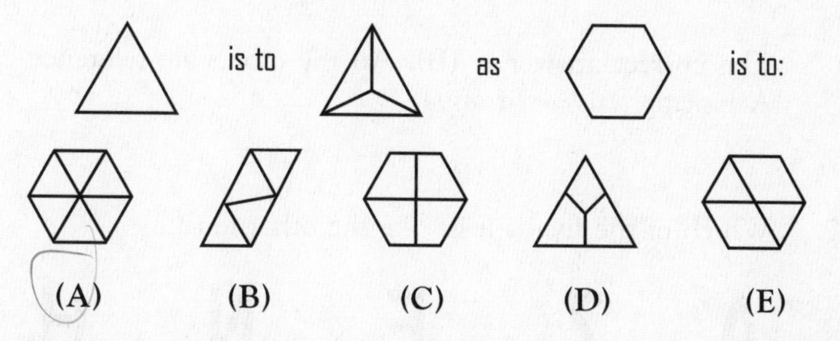

The correct answer is (A). The six-sided hexagon is divided into six equal parts by lines drawn from its outside vertices, just as the three-sided triangle is divided into three equal parts by lines drawn from its outside vertices.

4. Which of the five designs is least like the other four?

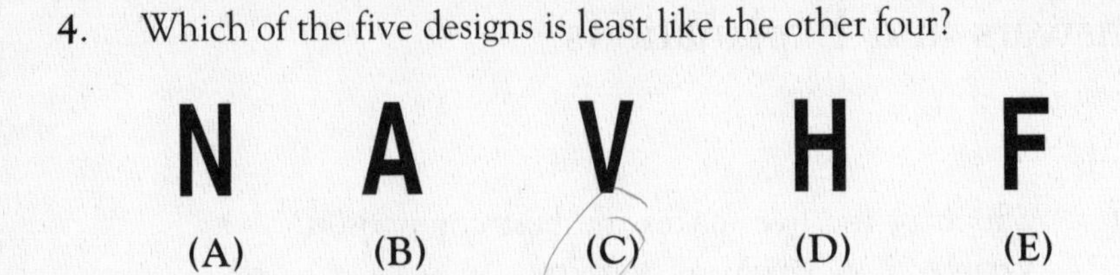

The correct answer is (C). All the others are made with three lines; V is made with two lines.

5. Jerry received both the fifteenth highest and the fifteenth lowest mark in the class. How many students are in the class?

15	25	29	30	32
(A)	(B)	(C)	(D)	(E)

The correct answer is (C). There are 14 students higher and 14 students lower. Jerry is the one in the middle, which makes him one of 29 students.

6. Which of the five is least like the other four?

DICTIONARY	BIOGRAPHY	ATLAS	ALMANAC	DIRECTORY
(A)	(B)	(C)	(D)	(E)

The correct answer is (B). All the others are reference books. A biography is a narrative.

7. Which of the five is least like the other four?

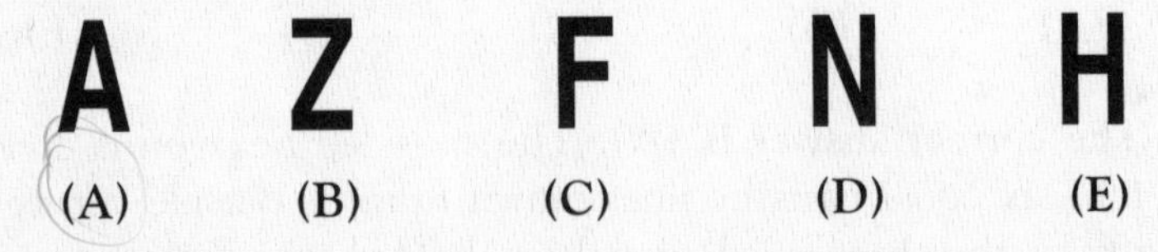

(A) (B) (C) (D) (E)

The correct answer is (A). The others are consonants; A is a vowel.

8. Which of the five makes the best comparison?
 Foot is to hand as leg is to:

ELBOW	PIANO	TOE	FINGER	ARM
(A)	(B)	(C)	(D)	(E)

The correct answer is (E). A foot is attached to a leg; a hand is attached to an arm.

9. Which of the five designs makes the best comparison?

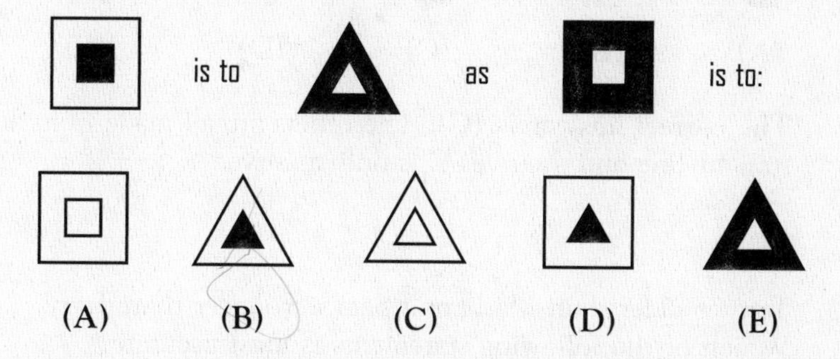

The correct answer is (B). The square changes to a triangle, and the shading is reversed.

10. If all Ferpies are Worgs and no Worgs are Sprickles, then no Sprickles are definitely Ferpies.
 This statement is definitely:

TRUE	FALSE	NEITHER
(A)	(B)	(C)

The correct answer is (A). Example: If all dogs are animals and no animals are plants, then no plants are definitely dogs.

11. Of the following numbers, which one is least like the others?

1 3 5 7 11 13 15 17 19

The correct answer is 15. The others are prime numbers—they can be divided only by themselves and 1. Fifteen is not a prime number. It can be divided by itself, 1, 3, and 5.

12. Which of the five designs is least like the other four?

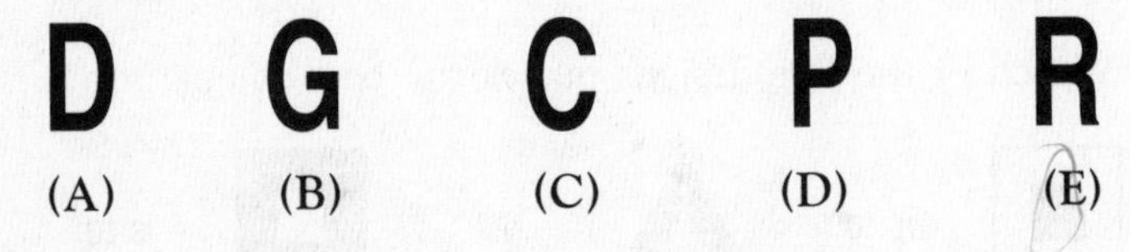

(A) (B) (C) (D) (E)

The correct answer is (C). The others are all made from a straight line and a curve. C is only a curve.

13. Terry is older than Mark, and Sam is younger than Terry. Which of the following statements is most accurate?

(A) Sam is older than Mark.
(B) Sam is younger than Mark.
(C) Sam is as old as Mark.
(D) It is impossible to tell whether Sam or Mark is older.

The correct answer is (D). Without more information, it is impossible to tell. We know only that both Mark and Sam are younger than Terry.

14. Which of the five designs is least like the other four?

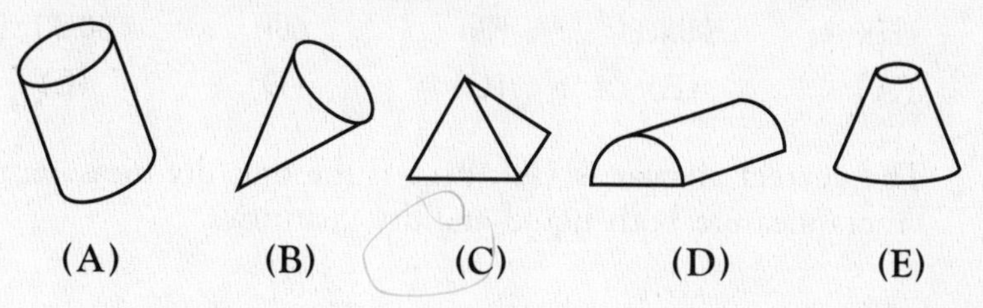

(A)	(B)	(C)	(D)	(E)

The correct answer is (C). It is made with only straight lines. The others are made with straight lines and curves.

15. Which of the five makes the best comparison?

Leap is to peal as 8326 is to:

2368	6283	2683	6328	3628
(A)	(B)	(C)	(D)	(E)

The correct answer is (D). Substitute numbers for letters: L = 8, E = 3, A = 2, P = 6. Thus, peal = 6328.

16. Anne received $0.59 in change from a supermarket purchase. Of the eleven coins she received in change, three were exactly alike. These three coins had to be:

PENNIES	NICKELS	DIMES	QUARTERS	HALF DOLLARS
(A)	(B)	(C)	(D)	(E)

The correct answer is (B). Four dimes, three nickels, and four pennies is the only solution.

17. Which of the five is least like the other four?

PECK	OUNCE	PINT	CUP	QUART
(A)	(B)	(C)	(D)	(E)

The correct answer is (A). Peck is the only dry measure; the others measure both liquid and dry quantities.

18. Three enemy messages were intercepted at communications headquarters. The code was broken, and it was found that "Berok tenlis krux" means "Secret attack Wednesday," and "Baroom zax tenlis" means "Secret plans included," and "Gradnor berok plil elan" means "Wednesday victory is ours." What does "krux" mean?

SECRET	WEDNESDAY	NOTHING	ATTACK	PLANS
(A)	(B)	(C)	(D)	(E)

The correct answer is (D). tenlis = secret; berok = Wednesday; krux = attack.

19. Which of the five makes the best comparison?

Love is to hate as valor is to:

COURAGE	SECURITY	COWARDICE	ANGER	TERROR
(A)	(B)	(C)	(D)	(E)

The correct answer is (C). Love is the opposite of hate. Valor is the opposite of cowardice.

20. The price of an article was cut 50% for a sale. By what percent must the price of the item be increased to again sell the item at the original price?

25%	50%	75%	100%	200%
(A)	(B)	(C)	(D)	(E)

The correct answer is (D). Example: A $20.00 item cut 50% will sell for $10.00. To again sell for $20.00, the item must be increased by $10.00, which is 100% of $10.00.

21. Which of the five designs makes the best comparison?

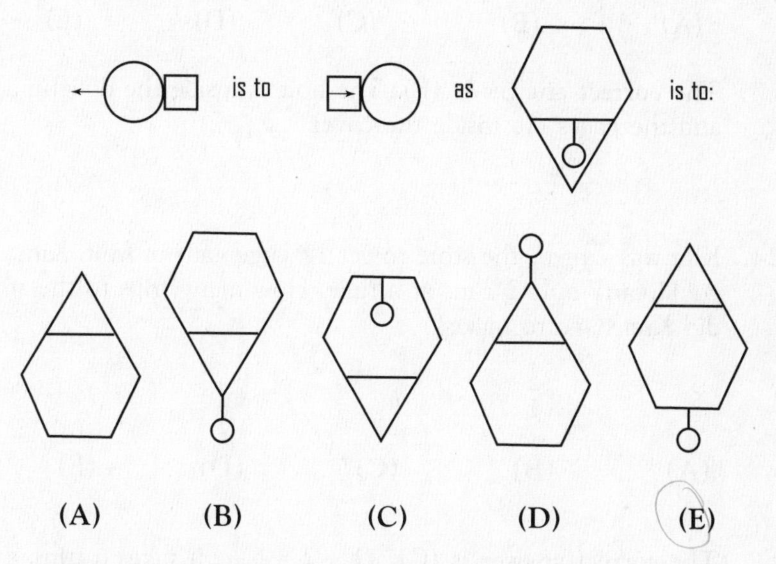

(A) (B) (C) (D) (E)

The correct answer is (E). The position of the geometric figures is reversed. The line figuration remains on the same side of the configuration, but is reversed.

22. Which of the five is least like the other four?

SQUASH	PUMPKIN	TOMATO	CUCUMBER	CORN
(A)	(B)	(C)	(D)	(E)

The correct answer is (E). Corn. The others grow on vines. Corn grows on a stalk.

23. Which of the five makes the best comparison?

Hole is to donut as pages are to:

STORY	WORDS	CONTENTS	INDEX	COVER
(A)	(B)	(C)	(D)	(E)

The correct answer is (E). The hole is inside the doughnut, and the pages are inside the cover.

24. Kim was sent to the store to get 11 large cans of fruit. Kim could carry only 2 cans at a time. How many trips to the store did Kim have to make?

5	$5\frac{1}{2}$	6	$6\frac{1}{2}$	7
(A)	(B)	(C)	(D)	(E)

The correct answer is (C). $11 \div 2 = 5\frac{1}{2}$. It takes 6 trips; a half trip won't get the last can home.

25. Which of the five designs makes the best comparison?

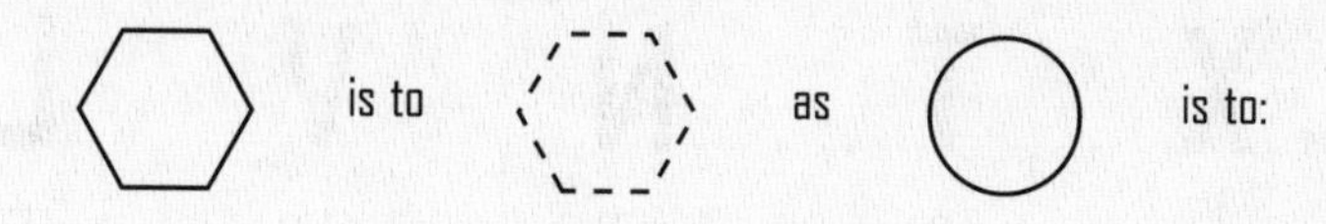

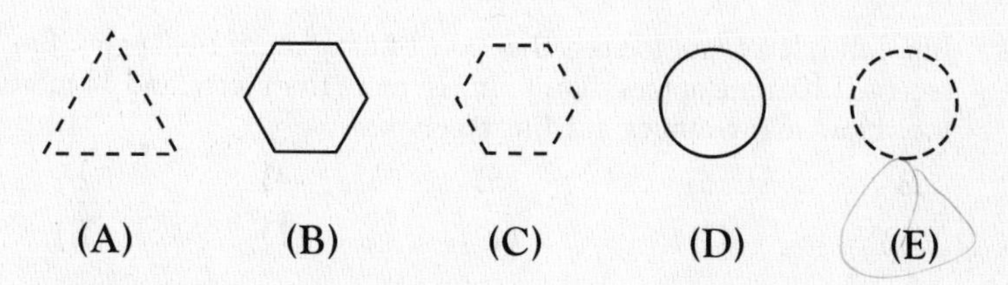

The correct answer is (E). It is a comparison of the same figure, solid to broken line.

26. If all Pleeps are Floops and all Floops are Leepies, then all Pleeps are definitely Leepies.

This statement is definitely:

TRUE	FALSE	NEITHER
(A)	(B)	(C)

The correct answer is (A). Example: "If all dogs are mammals and all mammals are animals, then all dogs are definitely animals."

27. Which of the five designs is least like the other four?

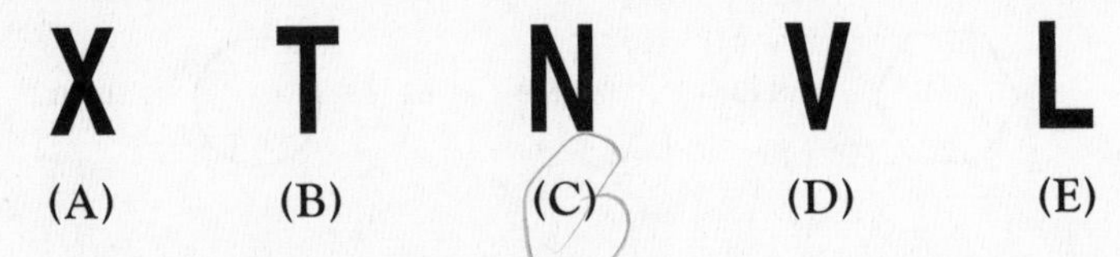

(A) (B) (C) (D) (E)

The correct answer is (C). All the others are made with two lines; N is made with three lines.

28. Jim, John, Jerry, and Joe together bought a basket of 144 apples. Jim received 10 more apples than John, 26 more than Jerry, and 32 more than Joe. How many apples did Jim receive?

73	63	53	43	27
(A)	(B)	(C)	(D)	(E)

The correct answer is (C). Jim received 53; John received 53 – 10 or 43; Jerry received 53 – 26 or 27; Joe received 53 – 32 or 21. 53 + 43 + 27 + 21 = 144. This problem may be solved algebraically as well.

29. Which of the five is least like the other four?

TOUCH	SEE	HEAR	EAT	SMELL
(A)	(B)	(C)	(D)	(E)

The correct answer is (D). The others are senses; eating is a body function.

30. Which of the five makes the best comparison?

Daughter is to father as niece is to:

NEPHEW	COUSIN	UNCLE	MOTHER	BROTHER
(A)	(B)	(C)	(D)	(E)

The correct answer is (C). Daughter is the female child of father; niece is the female child of uncle.

31. Which of the five designs is least like the other four?

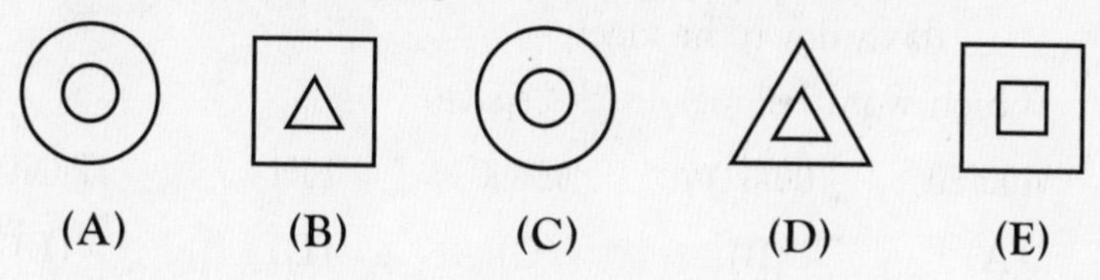

The correct answer is (B). The small figure inside the other figures is the same as the large figure it is inside.

32. Which number does not belong in the following series?

4 5 8 10 11 16 19 32 36

The correct answer is 11. The order is plus one, double the first figure; plus two, double the third figure; plus three, double the fifth figure; plus four.

33. Which of the five makes the best comparison?

Bark is to tree as scales are to:

GILLS	ELEPHANT	BUTCHER	FISH	SKIN
(A)	(B)	(C)	(D)	(E)

The correct answer is (D). Bark is on the outside of a tree; scales are on the outside of a fish.

34. Which if the five is least like the other four?

TURKEY	DUCK	CHICKEN	PHEASANT	GOOSE
(A)	(B)	(C)	(D)	(E)

The correct answer is (D). The others are or can be domesticated; pheasant is wild.

35. The secher vlooped quaply berak the kriggly lool. Then the secher _____ flaxly down the kleek.

Which word belongs in the space?

VLOOPED	QUAPLY	BERAK	LOOL	KRIGGLY
(A)	(B)	(C)	(D)	(E)

The correct answer is (A). A verb must go in the space. Example: The teacher walked quickly toward the open door. Then the teacher walked quickly down the hall.

36. The fish has a head 9 inches long. The tail is equal to the size of the head plus one half the size of the body. The body is the size of the head plus the tail. How long is the fish?

27 inches	54 inches	63 inches	72 inches	81 inches
(A)	(B)	(C)	(D)	(E)

The correct answer is (D). The head is 9 inches. The tail is 18 inches + 9 inches = 27 inches. The body is 9 inches + 19 inches + 9 inches = 36 inches. 9 inches + 27 inches + 36 inches = 72 inches. This may be solved algebraically as well.

37. Which of the five designs is least like the other four?

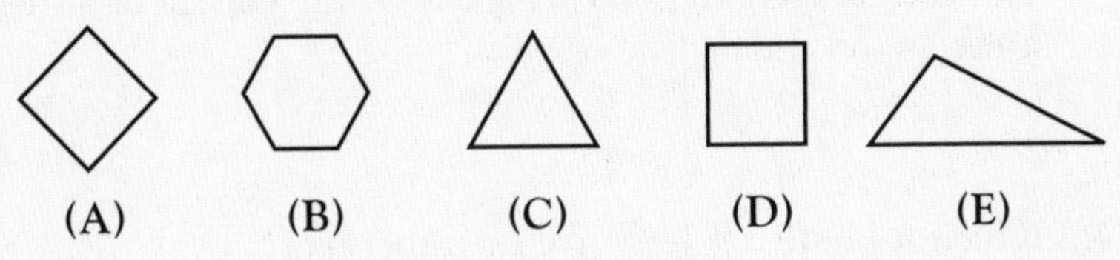

(A) (B) (C) (D) (E)

The correct answer is (E). All the other figures are symmetrical.

38. If you rearrange the letters in "NAICH," you would have the name of a(n):

COUNTRY	OCEAN	STATE	CITY	ANIMAL
(A)	(B)	(C)	(D)	(E)

The correct answer is (A). "NAICH" = "CHINA"

39. Jack is 15 years old, three times as old as his sister. How old will Jack be when he is twice as old as his sister?

18	20	24	26	30
(A)	(B)	(C)	(D)	(E)

The correct answer is (B). Jack is ten years older than his sister. In five years, Jack will be 20, and his sister who is now 5 will be 10.

40. Which of the five designs makes the best comparison?

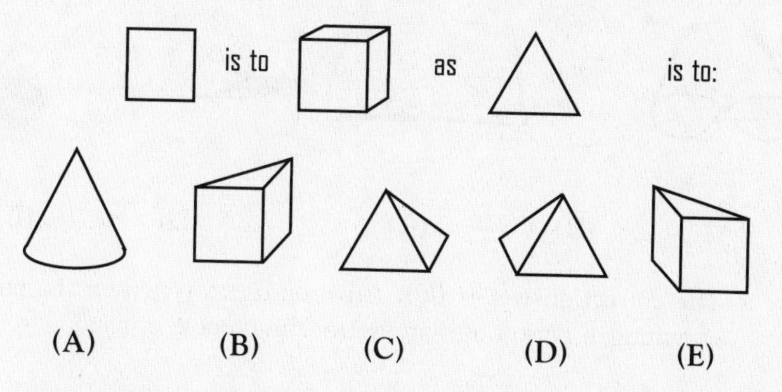

The correct answer is (C). The square is a direct frontal view of the cube that is then seen from the right. The triangle is a direct frontal view of the pyramid then seen from the right.

41. Slok are more zitful than mulk, but pringling flex are most _______ of all.

Which word belongs in the blank space?

SLOK	ZITFUL	MULK	PRINGLING	FLEX
(A)	(B)	(C)	(D)	(E)

The correct answer is (B). An adverb is required. Example: Nickels are more valuable than pennies, but twenty dollars are most valuable of all.

42. Which of the five makes the best comparison?

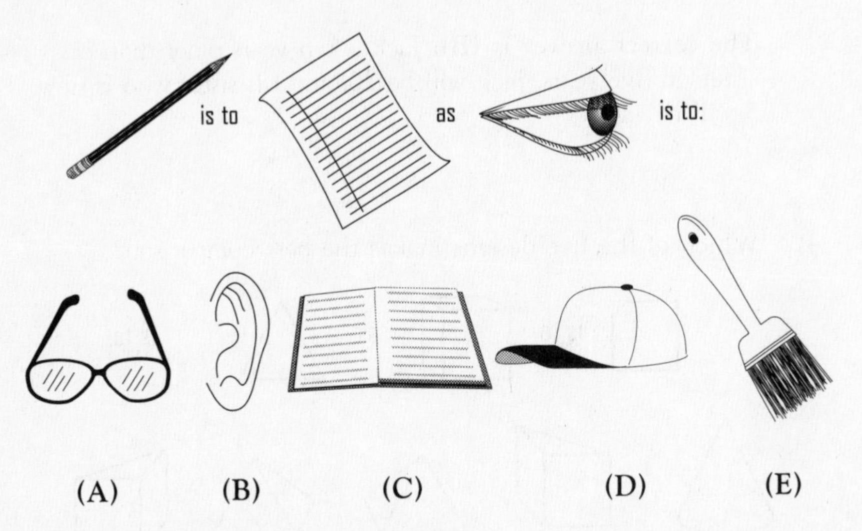

The correct answer is (C). A person uses a pencil for the purpose of writing; a person uses an eye for the purpose of reading.

43. If you rearrange the letters in "SHORE," you would have the name of a(n):

COUNTRY	OCEAN	STATE	CITY	ANIMAL
(A)	(B)	(C)	(D)	(E)

The correct answer is (E). "SHORE" = "HORSE"

44. Which number does not belong in the following series?

1 3 5 7 9 11 12 13 15

The correct answer is 12. The series is made from counting by twos.

45. Which of the five makes the best comparison?

Gas is to car as food is to:

MOUTH	STOMACH	ENERGY	BODY	TEETH
(A)	(B)	(C)	(D)	(E)

The correct answer is (D). Gas provides energy for a car; food provides energy for a body.

46. Which of the five designs is least like the other four?

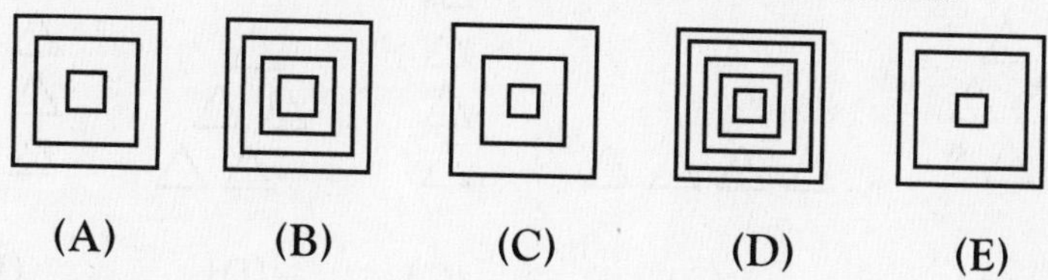

(A) (B) (C) (D) (E)

The correct answer is (B). All the others have an odd number of squares; choice (B) has an even number.

47. Which of the five is least like the other four?

WICHITA	DALLAS	CANTON	BANGOR	FRESNO
(A)	(B)	(C)	(D)	(E)

The correct answer is (A). All the others have six letters; Wichita has seven.

48. If some Tripples are Tropples and all Bolars are Tropples, then some Tripples are definitely Bolars.

This statement is:

TRUE	FALSE	NEITHER
(A)	(B)	(C)

The correct answer is (B). Example: "If some cars are green and all leaves are green, then some cars are definitely leaves."

49. Which of the five designs makes the best comparison?

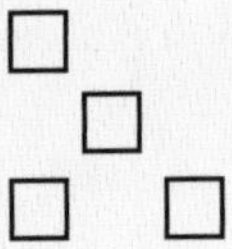

is to 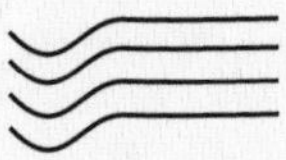 as 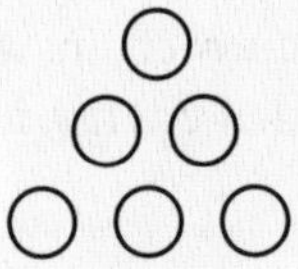 is to:

(A)  (B)  (C)  (D)  (E)

The correct answer is (E). Four figures change into four figures. Six figures change into six figures.

50. Which of the five makes the best comparison?

Light is to moon as book is to:

TACK	CHECK	TURF	BURN	TOY
(A)	(B)	(C)	(D)	(E)

The correct answer is (B). Moon can be combined with light to make the word "moonlight." Check can be combined with book to make the word "checkbook."

51. Which of the five designs is least like the other four?

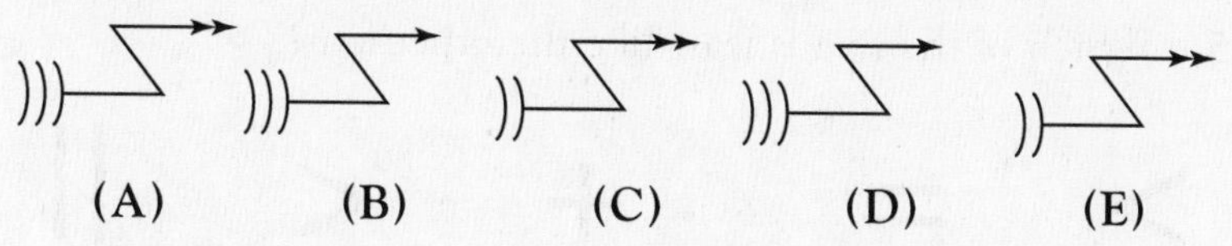

(A) (B) (C) (D) (E)

The correct answer is (A). It does not have a twin.

52. Which letter does not belong in the following series?

B E H K M N Q T

The correct answer is M. The series is made up of every fourth letter of the alphabet starting with B.

53. Which of the five makes the best comparison?

Pillow is to pillowcase as arm is to:

BODY	SLEEVE	HAND	GLOVE	RING
(A)	(B)	(C)	(D)	(E)

The correct answer is (B). A pillow fits inside a pillowcase. An arm fits inside a sleeve.

54. Which of the five is least like the other four?

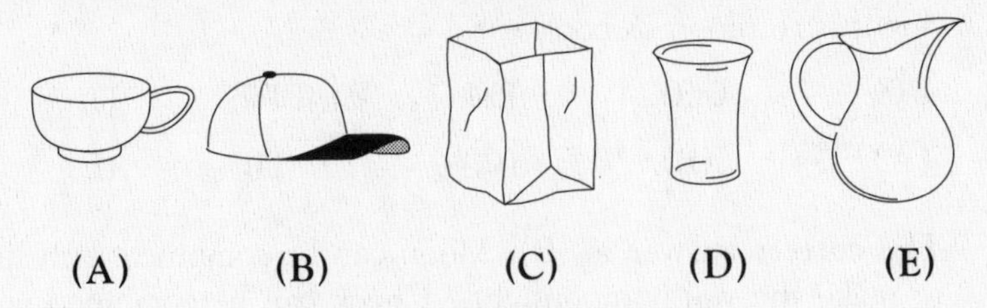

The correct answer is (B). All the others hold something inside. The cap fits on top of a head.

55. Which of the five is least like the other four?

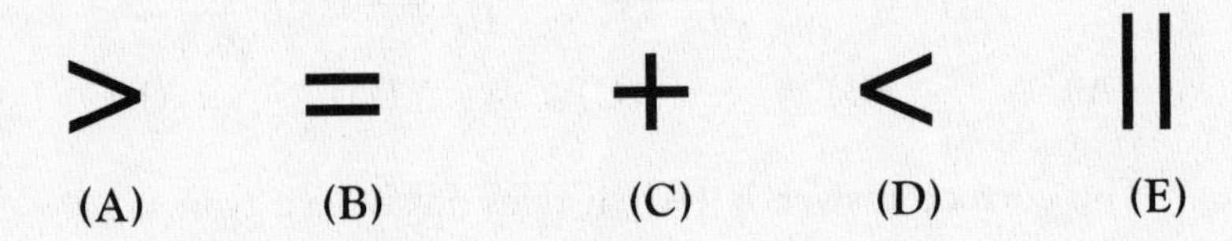

The correct answer is (C). The others all show mathematical relationships. + is a mathematical operation.

56. If all Truples are Glogs and some Glogs are Glips, then some Truples are definitely Glips.

This statement is:

TRUE	FALSE	NEITHER
(A)	(B)	(C)

The correct answer is (B). Example: "If all cats are animals and some animals are dogs, then some cats are definitely dogs."

57. If you rearrange the letters in "TALCATIN," you would have the name of a(n):

COUNTRY	OCEAN	STATE	CITY	ANIMAL
(A)	(B)	(C)	(D)	(E)

The correct answer is (B). "TALCATIN" = "ATLANTIC"

58. Which of the five is least like the other four?

ARTIST	GOLFER	NEWSCASTER	DANCER	MECHANIC
(A)	(B)	(C)	(D)	(E)

The correct answer is (C). All the others must use their hands and/or body but not words to perform their jobs. The newscaster must use words.

59. Which of the five does not belong in the series?

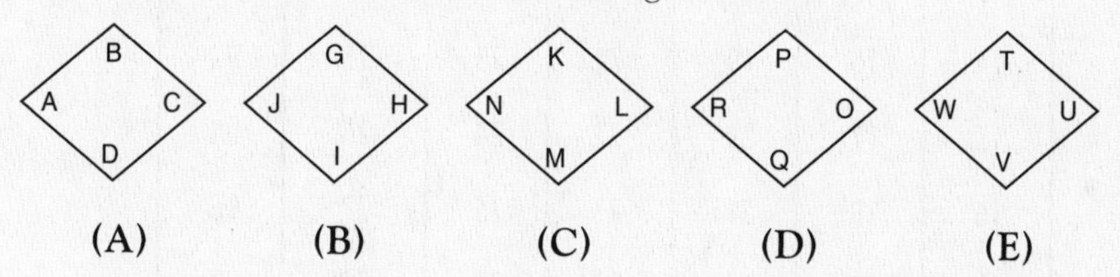

The correct answer is (D). The others have a sequence of letters in alphabetical order starting at the top and going clockwise.

60. Which of the five is least like the other four?

WATER	SUN	GASOLINE	WIND	CEMENT
(A)	(B)	(C)	(D)	(E)

The correct answer is (E). The others can all be used as sources of energy.

Scoring Instructions

Count up the number of questions you answered correctly. Find that number in the column appropriate to your age and circle the number. Then, directly to the right in the IQ column, you will locate your correct IQ rating. For example, if you are 14 years old and had 32 answers correct, you locate 32 in the 14-year-old column and find that you have an IQ rating of 114.

		AGE			16+	I.Q.
11	12	13	14	15	Adult	
8	10	13	15	17	19	80
9	11	14	16	18	20	82
10	12	15	17	19	21	84
11	13	16	18	20	22	86
12	14	17	19	21	23	88
13	15	18	20	22	24	90
14	16	19	21	23	25	92
15	17	20	22	24	26	94
16	18	21	23	25	27	96
17	19	22	24	26	28	98
18	20	23	25	27	29	100
19	21	24	26	28	30	102
20	22	25	27	29	31	104
21	23	26	28	30	32	106
22	24	27	29	31	33	108
23	25	28	30	32	34	110
24	26	29	31	33	35	112

AGE						I.Q.
11	12	13	14	15	16+ Adult	
25	27	30	32	34	36	114
26	28	31	33	35	37	116
27	29	32	34	36	38	118
28	30	33	35	37	39	120
29	31	34	36	38	40	122
30	32	35	37	39	41	124
31	33	36	38	40	42	126
32	34	37	39	41	43	128
33	35	38	40	42	44	130
34	36	39	41	43	45	132
35	37	40	42	44	46	134
36	38	41	43	45	47	136
37	39	42	44	46	48	138
38	40	43	45	47	49	140
39	41	44	46	48	50	142
40	42	45	47	49	51	144
41	43	46	48	50	52	146
42	44	47	49	51	53	148
43	45	48	50	52	54	150
44	46	49	51	53	55	154
45	47	50	52	54	56	158
46	48	51	53	55	57	160
47	49	52	54	56	58+	165+

part 2

Intelligence—What It Is and What It Means

What Your Score Means

The first indicator of your intelligence is that you have taken this test. Curiosity already reveals a higher level of overall intelligence. It also reveals that you are motivated enough to pursue your interests.

In the past, IQ scores were usually kept secret or at least well guarded. There was some justification for not sharing the results openly. However, the public is more educated now regarding what the scores mean and what they measure, so the information can now be understood and used.

An informed person weighs data or information within the context of other facts. If someone gave you a choice of two gold bars, one that is one inch wide and the other five inches wide, which would you choose? Certainly, you couldn't make a wise decision based only on the information given. You need more information. How high and how deep are the bars? What does each bar weigh? Those answers would give you a better understanding of the value of the choices. The same is true of an IQ score. Your IQ as an indicator can be useful for evaluation, but it is not the only indicator of a person's value.

Let's explore how your IQ score relates to the many others who have taken this test. The following graph shows the distribution of intelligence among the general population. It reveals where you stand in relation to other people. The numbers given on the bottom are IQ levels. The left shows the percentage of people in the population with that score. The categories of what the IQ scores mean are shown at the top. Among authorities, the division of the categories and their names given may vary slightly, but they generally agree.

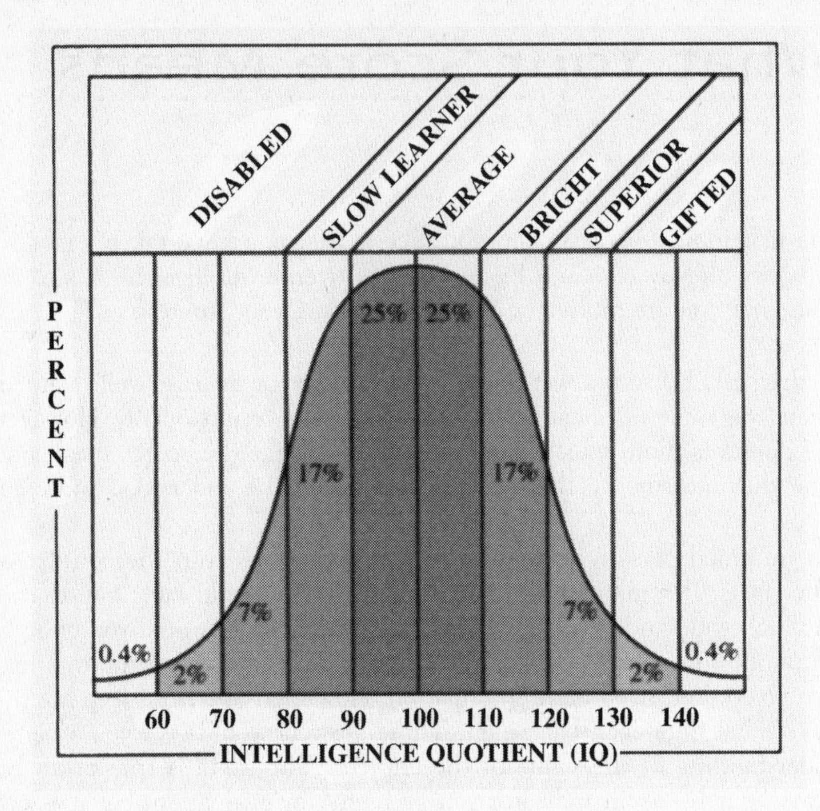

The graph shows the classic bell-shaped curve. Based on mathematical laws of probability, the bell curve closely reflects the conditions found in actual life. For example, if you take 100 people and measure their height, of the hundred, about 50 people will have an average height. Some will be taller and some will be shorter, but the number of those will be less than the number who are of average height. In addition, there will be only a few people who are very tall or very short.

Psychometrics is an area of study that uses testing to measure aspects of mental processes. Psychometric studies revealed that about 50 percent of the population have IQ test scores that fall into the middle of the bell curve. This means that most people of the population have an IQ in the range between 90 and 109, which is average intelligence. Use the graph to see where you fit in relation to the rest of the population.

The graph shows that a score between 110 and 119 indicates bright intelligence. A score between 120 and 129 denotes superior intelligence, and a score of 130 or over reveals giftedness. Some tests divide superior and giftedness at 135 and above, while others place it at 140 and above. A score over 160 reveals a superior giftedness, which is in the genius category. Generally, one out of every 160 people has an IQ of 140, but one in 11,000 has an IQ of 160!

Even as a genius, the critical factor of intelligence is its development and use. Without development, application, and productivity, high intelligence is a valueless characteristic, both to the individual and to society. In the same way, an IQ between 80 and 89 reveals a slow learner category, and scores under 80 indicate a degree of mental handicap. However, an IQ score primarily expresses the mental abilities needed for a person's success in a traditional school situation. Individuals with lower IQ scores can still enjoy a full life and be productive members of society.

The results of one test may not indicate a true level of intelligence or potential capability. Therefore, one IQ test score should not be used to label or place an individual in a permanent school or life setting, especially if the score is in the extreme high or low range. Evaluate patterns of scores against other factors, such as behavior, interests, thinking style, and actual production. For IQ scores to be most meaningful, an established pattern of test scores over a certain period of time is best. Therefore, it is important for youngsters to be present each time a test is administered in school.

There are some things to note when considering this score or a range of scores. Normally, scores vary on occasion and among different tests. The variance may be from 10 points above to 10 points below your actual IQ. This margin of error can occur because emotional and physical states and other factors vary from day to day. The amount of sleep you get the night before, testing conditions, and more are all factors. Consider your state of mind before and during the test. If a person thinks that they aren't going to do well on the test, it can affect the outcome.

Also, some may see an IQ test as intimidating because of its weight and importance. Another may see the test as a confirmation of a negative label placed upon them.

Evolution of IQ Test Scoring

In 1904, Albert Binet and Theodore Simon needed a way to identify French children who did not function as well in the usual school setting. They wanted to find children who needed more help and instruction to learn. Therefore, the areas that Binet tested related more to traditional academic and scholastic abilities than other skills or potential.

Creativity, motor skills, spatial perceptions, and so forth were not included. Though Binet set the tone and course for this type of testing, he had a wider view of intelligence. He viewed intelligence as a complimentary group of perceptions and abilities and created many tests to measure them. However, the test he used to identify academic abilities is the one he is known for and the one that has been copied and used more widely than any other.

Binet and Simon assigned a score that designated the mental age (MA) of a student. In 1916, Lewis A. Terman developed a version of Binet's test in the United States. It has been improved since, but it still plays a major role as an academic identifier. It is also used as a predictor of academic success. Terman improved the scoring when he used the chronological age (CA), which is the actual age in years, to divide the mental age (MA), which is the number of correct answers. The MA is determined by the test responses of many people. Scientists analyze test questions to find which questions people of a certain age can expect to answer successfully. After considerable statistical analysis, tests are "normed" or "standardized" by administering questions designated "age level" to many individuals of that age.

Thus, IQ equals the MA divided by the CA. The resulting score is multiplied by 100, so any score with a decimal portion is expressed in hundreds. For example, a score of 1.12 becomes an IQ of 112, and a score of 1.54 is shown as an IQ of 154.

$$IQ = MA/CA \times 100$$

For example, how many correct answers do 10 year olds give to items considered to be problems that an average 10 year old should be able to solve? If a 10 year old takes the test and correctly completes the items a 10 year old should be able to do, but no more, that indicates a mental age of 10. See the following formula:

$$IQ = 10/10 \times 100$$

$$IQ = 1.0 \times 100$$

$$IQ = 100$$

As another example, a 10 year old answers all the items that a 10 year old should be able to do and then all the items a 13 year old should be able to do. That individual has a mental age of 13. See the following formula:

$$IQ = 13/10 \times 100$$

$$IQ = 1.3 \times 100$$

$$IQ = 130$$

What Is Intelligence?

Intelligence is unseen, yet you can see its effects, and you can measure its effects. The fact that you cannot see it does not mean that it is not real or that it is not important. Scientists attempt to identify attributes of intelligence as reflected through intelligent behavior. We can observe intelligent behavior and intelligent performance.

Intelligence, though a widely used concept in psychology, is still undefined. Defining it has kept scientists busy throughout the past century. Perhaps the greatest sign of where we are in successfully defining overall intelligence is in viewing the thoughts of the great minds of the twentieth century. The opinions of the scientists, psychologists, and sociologists who have studied overall intelligence are extremely diverse.

While each scientist has his or her own unique concept and definition of intelligence, most agree on certain common abilities. Intelligence is ability or skill and an adaptability to resolve new problems that tends to remain relatively constant throughout life. However, with exercise, it is possible to increase your IQ score and to take greater advantage of the intelligence you have.

Some have attributed the following statement to Alfred Binet, but psychological historian Edwin G. Boring said it after struggling with the definition of intelligence. In desperation, Boring concluded that intelligence is what intelligence tests measure. It is a simple enough definition, but it doesn't completely define intelligence. It falls short because there are many well-respected IQ tests, but the areas they test sometimes differ.

In its simplest form, intelligence is the ability to logically think and reason and to resolve problems effectively. Wechsler, the developer of the Wechsler Adult Intelligence Scale-Revised (WAIS-R) and the third edition of the Wechsler Intelligence Scale for Children (WISC III) defined intelligence as, ". . . the aggregate or global capacity to act purposefully, to think rationally, and to deal effectively with [the] environment."

Other definitions imply speed, efficiency, and innate ability or potential. All of these are only partly correct. While some animals may be taught specific abilities, such as fetching or finding the way through a maze, few, if any, animals would score well on a general intelligence test. Intelligence separates humans from other forms of animal life.

> **Intelligence is characterized by a mental process that incorporates speed, efficiency, agility, and flexibility in the purposeful mental activity of dealing with life tasks, problem solving, and the production of both conventional and innovative ideas, services, and products. It requires not only the ability to apply attained skills but also the ability to acquire new ones.**
>
> **—Alfred W. Munzert**

When intelligence is studied or measured, what actually is observed is intelligent behavior or intelligent performance, not intelligence. Intelligent action is a product of intelligence.

If we think in terms of intelligent behavior rather than intelligence, it is easier to identify and build a basis for defining the abstract concept of intelligence.

For example, of the two behaviors shown in the pictures below, which do you think is more intelligent?

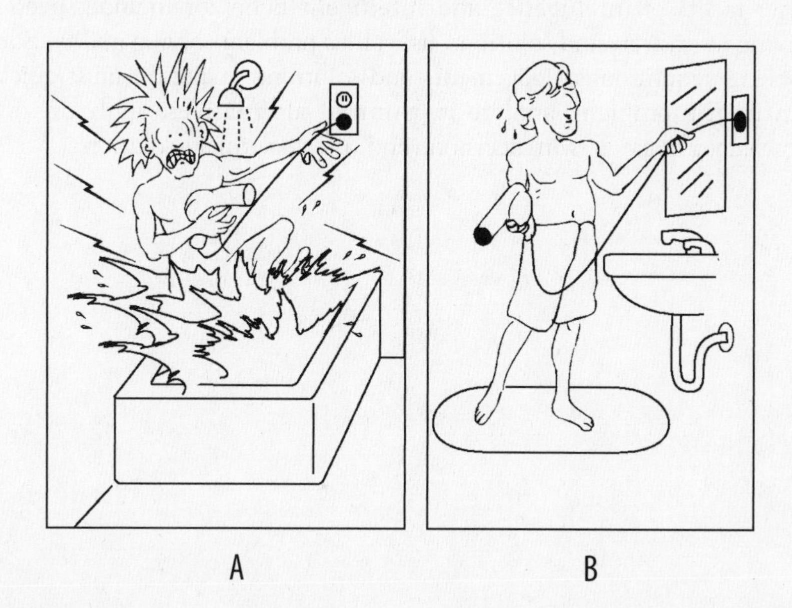

A B

Of course you chose the panel showing Actor B, whose behavior is far more intelligent than that of Actor A. You compared one behavior to a related behavior under the same set of circumstances. In order to do this, you had to have a basic storehouse of information about electricity, its nature, and its relationship to water. The process you went through to make an observation and judgment of intelligent behavior should give you some insight to the nature of intelligent behavior. The basis of intelligent behavior must be knowledge and information in its broadest sense. This information may have been acquired formally or informally.

We would not consider Actor A's behavior unintelligent if he were only two years old, but we might inquire about the intelligence of the parent who permitted the child to be in a position to act dangerously and without the information on which to act intelligently.

Memory is the underpinning of intelligent behavior. For instance, in the preceding example, someone must recall information about the dangerous nature of electricity in water in order to affect a behavior. Applying previous learning to current situations is a factor related to remembering information. This is the ability to transfer or to generalize. Some individuals have much more capacity for transfer than do others. Those who have this ability are usually significantly more intelligent than those who do not.

Other facets of intelligence and intelligent behavior include speed in arriving at answers and solutions, as well as problem-solving ability. Some problems require rapid judgements and solutions. A person must quickly identify the problem, analyze it, think of alternatives, apply previous knowledge, make a swift decision, and affect a timely solution.

IQ and Its Importance

You should know your IQ score and use it to evaluate yourself, but be sure to maintain some objectivity. For some individuals, knowing their IQ is just what they need to bolster themselves and give themselves the confidence to attempt new things or to tax their mental resources and stretch them to reach greater heights. For others, it may have the opposite effect. Learning that one's IQ is below normal may be devastating. Other people wear their IQ score like a badge that frees them from any real productivity. They may feel that they don't have to try very hard. However, being smart does not ensure success.

In the last half of the twentieth century, educators used a student's IQ to evaluate their potential and place them into the proper educational environment. Using an IQ score for that purpose makes good sense. IQ scores are important because within our society, schools, universities, employers, the military, and the public place a premium value on intelligence. We sometimes view the score as more important than achievement, motivation, and the actual ability to deal effectively in the real world. Some scientists believe the aspects tested by the traditional IQ test are the "core" of intelligence. They see them as an innate ability and potential, while others believe the tests cover only a few of the many aspects of intelligence.

There is controversy among educators and parents over the use of intelligence scores. Much of the controversy is over the misuse of IQ tests. Any long-term decisions about educational needs or placement in an educational setting should consider a series of IQ scores along with a host of other behaviors that aren't identified through such tests. Too often, children have been incorrectly labeled as having less ability and/or potential than they actually possess. As a result, they end up in limiting educational settings.

Some children are placed above their abilities. While it is good to stretch one's limits within reason, being placed too highly can add considerable stress on children as they attempt to keep up with their peers.

Where a student is placed is not the only problem. IQ scores can affect a child's future success. Especially as a child, you tend to believe others' assessment of you, and, consciously or unconsciously, you end up living as though it were true.

A low score on an intelligence test may signal that a child needs different methods of instruction. A learning-disabled child who does not receive early remedial assistance and instruction in school will very likely show a test pattern of decreasing test scores between entering school and the sixth grade. The child may be quite intelligent, but because of poor language and math skills, the child may learn and test like a slow learner. These children with unique needs now have access to different kinds of instruction and instructional media.

IQ scores are important to society as a whole. Legislatures, schools and universities, sociologists, employers, and industries use intelligence research. For better or worse, they want to set the course for society in the future.

Understanding Left-Brain and Right-Brain Functions

Recent research on the differences between left-brain and right-brain functions has shed new light on the relationship between intelligence and creativity. Each half of the brain functions differently and processes information differently. Wolfgang Luthe, in *Creativity Mobilization Technique* (1976), characterizes left-brain thinking as "spotlight thinking" and right-brain thinking as "floodlight" thinking.

The left hemisphere controls the mental functions that include memory, language, logic, computation, seriation, classification, writing, analysis, and convergent thinking. These are the skills and abilities necessary for success in a traditional academic setting. They are also the primary skills focused on in intelligence tests. See the following figure.

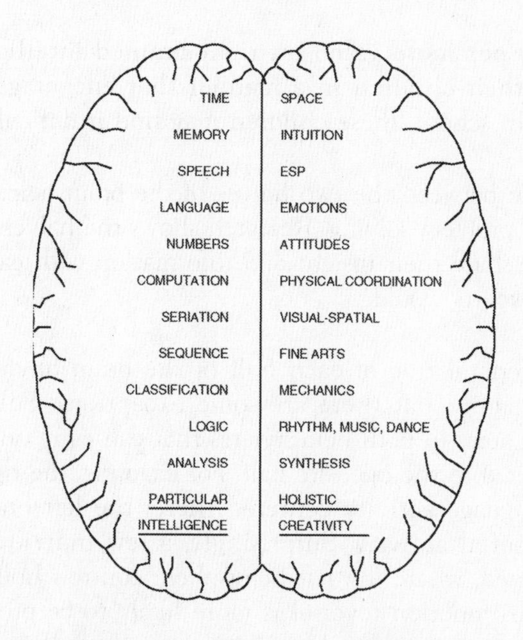

Mental Activities of Each Hemisphere

The right hemisphere is the control center for the mental functions involved in intuition, attitudes and emotions, visual and spatial relationships, music, rhythm, dance, physical coordination and activity, synthesis, and divergent thinking processes. The left-brain functions are sequential and orderly. In comparison, the right-brain functions are holistic and diffuse. The left brain sees the parts and organizes them into a whole; the right brain sees the whole, then the parts. Left-brain thinking is the essence of academic success and intelligence as it is now measured. Right-brain thinking is the essence of creativity.

The two hemispheres must function in a balanced and integrated manner to allow wholesome human functioning and a successful balance in mental and physical health. Our society is a left-brained society, and our schools emphasize and promote left-brain mental activity at the expense of the development of the right-brained functions.

We have excluded the holistic and creative right-brain functions. Thus, individuals who are dominantly right-brained thinkers find most classroom and community settings challenging.

Some families put more value on right-brained intelligence. Those families raise their children in a manner that encourages right-brain development. In school, these children may find it difficult to adjust.

A good balance between the two halves of the brain helps in successful and intelligent problem solving. Research shows the halves are not independent. They share their insight and information with each other, just as a team of experts would.

Overall, the general rule of each half of the brain having a different function does apply, but there are some exceptions. Scientists found small or minor areas in both hemispheres that can carry on the activities generally centered in the opposite half. For example, the right brain may have some language activity centered there; the left brain may have some visual-spatial activity. Surprisingly, a few individuals have the functions reversed, where the left hemisphere controls holistic thinking. Apparently, this function reversal is more likely to be present in ambidextrous people, who can use both hands equally well.

It is best to use both sides of the brain equally in order to achieve the most effective solutions. However, most people have a more dominant side of their brain that they use a little more. This is a problem only when one side is dominant enough to cause a reduced ability to live everyday life, solve problems, and learn. If you receive a low intelligence score and have had difficulty learning in a regular classroom, you may be a visual-spatial, holistic learner, rather than a slow learner. This is likely if you show evidence of good mental agility when dealing with problems that require physical action or the manipulation of objects, rather than ideas, for a solution.

Such a child may be functionally handicapped in a classroom setting. This is especially true where children receive instruction requiring them to use a predominantly left-brain mental process. That child not only has difficulty with traditional instruction, but also experiences frustration when most of that instruction is based solely on mastery of written and spoken language. This frustration could add further learning difficulties if the child views himself or herself as someone who cannot succeed.

Left Brain, Right Brain, and Your IQ Score

After your introduction to the right-brain, left-brain functions and distinctions, you are probably curious about where you fit in. The IQ test at the beginning of the book taps both left-brain and right-brain abilities.

You may have done extremely well on one type of question but not so well on the other. Most people find one type of question easier but have abilities in both areas. As noted in an earlier section of this book, it is not possible to construct a paper-and-pencil test that comprehensively tests the right-brain types of abilities. Most IQ tests examine areas of general knowledge, mathematical aptitude, vocabulary, memory, problem solving, and spatial perception. While most paper-and-pencil IQ tests are essentially tests for the left-brain functions, each specific item in the test can be analyzed for its left-brain, right-brain components, and, from this analysis, some interesting conclusions may be drawn.

We have carefully analyzed each specific question on this IQ test and have placed each into one of two categories. The first category contains the questions that test predominantly left-brain functions; the second category contains those questions that test both left- and right-brain functions. By identifying the questions that required right-brain processing, you may gain further insight into your own IQ score.

Return to your IQ test now and, on the analysis sheet (see the following page), list the left-brain questions that you missed under Category I and the right-brain questions that you got wrong under Category II. Carefully review all the questions from both categories that you had correct and, in the last column, list those questions from among your correct answers that were "just right guesses."

Left-Brain, Right-Brain Test Analysis

Category I Left Brain	Category II Right Brain	Guesses

Category I: Left-Brain Questions

1. Primarily a left-brain question that taps abilities in sequencing and analysis. It also requires the right-brain ability to recognize position in space.

2. A left-brain question tapping abilities in classification, analysis, general information, and memory.

5. A left-brain question requiring mathematical and sequencing skills.

6. A left-brain question tapping classification, memory, analysis, and general informational abilities.

7. A left-brain question requiring information, memory, analysis, and general informational abilities.

8. A left-brain question tapping classification, memory, information, and analysis skills.

10. A left-brain question tapping ability in logic and analysis.

11. A left-brain question requiring mathematical, informational, and memory skills.

13. A left-brain question requiring logic and analysis.

16. A left-brain question requiring numerical, mathematical, informational, memory, and analysis skills.

17. A left-brain question tapping classification, information, and memory.

18. A left-brain question requiring language and analysis skills.

20. A left-brain question tapping mathematical, informational, memory, and analysis skills.

22. A left-brain question requiring language, information, and memory. However, if you arrived at the answer through a mental picture of the garden where these vegetables grow, you are relying on right-brain processing in problem solving.

23. A left-brain question tapping classification, information, memory, analysis, and analogy.

24. A left-brain question requiring numerical and mathematical skills, information, and memory.

26. A left-brain question in logic and analysis. However, if you arrived at an answer by using a pictorial diagram, you are relying to a great extent on right-brain information processing.

28. A left-brain question requiring mathematical and analysis skills along with memory and general information.

29. A left-brain question tapping language, general information, memory, and classification.

30. A left-brain question tapping information, memory, analysis, and classification skills.

32. A left-brain question tapping mathematical, information, memory, sequencing, and analysis skills.

33. A left-brain question requiring language, information, classification, analysis, and memory skills.

34. A left-brain question requiring language, information, memory, classification, and analysis.

35. A left-brain question tapping language, classification, and analysis skills.

36. A left-brain question tapping mathematical, informational, memory, and analysis skills.

38. A left-brain question tapping language, sequencing, informational, memory, and classification skills. The right-brain position-in-space function is also related.

39. A left-brain question requiring mathematical, memory, informational, and analysis skills.

41. A left-brain question requiring language, classification, and analysis skills.

43. A left-brain question requiring language, information, sequencing, and analysis skills. The right-brain function of position-in-space also comes into play.

44. A left-brain skill requiring mathematical, informational, memory, sequencing, and analysis skills.

45. A left-brain question tapping information, memory, classification, and analysis abilities.

48. A left-brain question requiring logic and analysis skills.

50. A left-brain question tapping language, memory, and analysis abilities.

52. A left-brain question requiring language, information, memory, classification, and analysis skills.

53. A left-brain question tapping language, information, memory, classification, and analysis skills.

55. A left-brain question tapping mathematical, information, memory, and analysis skills.

56. A left-brain question tapping logic and analysis skills.

58. A left-brain question tapping language, information, classification, memory, and analysis abilities.

60. A left-brain question tapping language, classification, information, memory, and analysis abilities.

Category II: Right-Brain Questions

3. A right-brain question based on ability to see relationships in space-form. It also requires left-brain skills in classification.

4. This question taps both the right-brain skills in space-form and left-brain number skills.

9. A right-brain question requiring ability in space-form but also requiring left-brain skills in classification and analogy.

12. A right-brain question tapping abilities in space-form but also requiring left-brain skills in classification and analysis.

14. A right-brain question tapping abilities in space-form relationships but also requiring left-brain skills in classification and analysis.

15. A question tapping the right-brain abilities in spatial relationships but also requiring left-brain analysis and sequencing.

19. A question that is right brain in terms of the information with which it deals but left brain in that it taps abilities in vocabulary, analogy, and analysis.

21. A right-brain question dealing with space-form relationships but also requiring left-brain abilities of analysis and analogy.

22. A left-brain question requiring language, information, and memory. However, if you arrived at the answer through a mental picture of the garden where these vegetables grow, you are relying on right-brain processing in problem solving.

25. A right-brain question tapping abilities in space-form relationships that also requires left-brain skills of classification and analysis.

26. A left-brain question in logic and analysis. However, if you arrived at an answer by using a pictorial diagram, you are relying to a great extent on right-brain information processing.

27. A right-brain question tapping space-form relationships but also requiring left-brain numerical skills.

31. A right-brain question tapping informational, memory, analysis, and classification skills.

37. A right-brain question tapping abilities in space-form relationships and requiring left-brain classification and analysis.

40. A right-brain question tapping space-form relationship abilities and requiring left-brain skills in classification and analysis.

42. A combination of right- and left-brain skills. The question is based on the ability to gain information through visual images, but it requires the left-brain functions of information, memory, classification, and analysis.

46. A right-brain question requiring abilities in space-form relationships but also requiring left-brain skills in numbers.

47. A right-brain question requiring abilities in spatial relationships but also requiring left-brain number skills.

49. A right-brain question requiring abilities in space-form relationships but also tapping left-brain numerical skills and abilities in classification and analysis.

51. A right-brain question tapping space-form relationship skills but also requiring left-brain abilities in classification, numbers, and analysis.

54. A question based on ability to process right-brain visual-image information but requiring left-brain information, classification, and analysis skills.

57. A question that taps right-brain position-in-space abilities but that is heavily left brain in requiring language, information, memory, sequencing, and analysis skills.

59. A question that deals with right-brain position-in-space skills but which also requires left-brain language, sequencing, and information and analysis skills.

Interpreting Your Results

By comparing the three columns on page 69, we can come to a number of conclusions:

1. If you missed a fairly equal number of items from both those itemized as left brain and those characterized as right brain, then the possibility is that there is a dominance of neither right- nor left-brain processing. Your brain uses a balanced left- and right-brain processing in most problems you encounter.

2. If most of the questions that you missed fall into the second category (questions requiring right-brain processing), then the probability is that you are a left-brain–oriented individual who tends to approach and answer problems and questions primarily through left-brain processing.

3. If most of the questions that you missed are under the left-brain category, it may indicate that you are primarily or dominantly a right-brain thinker. If you did quite well on the questions that were based on or require right-brain skills but did not score particularly high on the test, you may well be an intelligent right-brain thinker. An in-depth individual test that is professionally administered and that includes "performance" type questions and problems would give you a better analysis of your abilities and of your IQ.

4. Take another look at the number of questions at which you guessed but which you answered correctly. These answers were arrived at through intuitive thinking, which is a right-brain process. It is most likely, especially if there are several of these, that they were not wild guesses but were arrived at through your right brain's intuitive function working with information stored deep in your left-brain memory bank. These answers, regardless of the category of the questions, indicate right-brain functioning.

This analysis of left- and right-brain functioning raises some interesting points. The questions on the IQ test that tap right-brain functions also require abilities that are essentially left brain. However, the reverse is not true. Most left-brain questions on the test that deal with language and numbers do not necessarily require right-brain abilities. We are thus able to identify and separate the questions into two categories.

Right-brain thinkers, when confronted with questions of language, logic, or mathematics—which are essentially left-brain problems—may use pictures or diagrams or may think in mental pictures in an effort to solve them. Or they "guess," which is an intuitive, right-brain response. In brief, they are applying right-brain processing to left-brain questions. Thus, the list of correct "guesses" on the test is a further strong indication of right-brain functioning. Although the analysis is far from precise, it gives you a good indication of whether you employ balanced or predominantly left- or right-brain processing in your approach to the problems confronting you in your everyday life.

Such insight might well be significant. If, for example, the indication is that you are predominantly left-brain oriented, perhaps you are overlooking or neglecting the development of some creative or artistic abilities you possess. If the indications are that you are predominantly right-brain oriented, then you are essentially a creative individual who tends to think holistically or in patterns and who may, therefore, have encountered past difficulties in a left-brain-oriented society.

Remember when you started some training or sport or began a job that required physical strength or agility? You didn't do it very well in the beginning. It took some practice. No one suddenly does 50 pushups if they haven't done any for a year. We realistically don't expect to be able to accomplish that.

Traditionally, scientists have viewed the left hemisphere as the dominant or major hemisphere and the right as the minor hemisphere. Now, the belief is that dominance of one hemisphere over another occurs essentially because of learning and mental exercise. It is not an inherent quality. Just as we naturally prefer to use our right or left hand, we don't exclude using the other. Society favors training the logical left-side brain functions, but we can expand the functionality of our right brain and encourage both hemispheres to work together. Each person can reap the benefits of exercising the brain and enjoy the added facility of a quick mind, with added creative abilities. Let us explore some methods of how to build up and keep your brain agile.

Read. Read to have fun, to learn, to understand, to empathize, and to entertain. Read to yourself and read to others, for your sake and theirs. Read aloud to your children, frequently, even after they are in their teens. For preschool and elementary children, it is a great influence. It triggers their desire to read and determines their success at it. Reading enhances their language skills and stimulates their ability to frame their thoughts in writing.

Use additional interactive methods to help you retain what you read. We all learn in many ways. Anytime you can use more than one gateway to your intellect and memory, the information flows in much faster. Reading retention and comprehension is increased by taking notes, discussing or narrating what was read, looking up the cited references, or highlighting passages. If possible, write a summary. A summary allows you to succinctly cement the knowledge into your memory. The summary doesn't need to be formal, but it should help you to recall the essence of a book or article.

Listening to someone read is much more of a mental activity than watching television. Having someone read to you exercises your auditory perception, your ability to pay attention, and your ability to conceptualize. It also stimulates your other creative abilities.

Neuroscientists are finding that activities that require someone to visualize and imagine stimulate growth of neural connections in those areas of the brain. As you listen and imagine, areas of your mind are strengthened and exercised, and new pathways are developed.

Everyone, especially adults, should listen to books on tape. In this mobile society, we spend a good deal of time in our cars. That time is used better in imagining, listening, and learning. Incredible actors read the stories and bring the books to life. The authors have strived to perfect the verbal tone and cadence of the words, and the actors heighten that sense as they read the story. This adds a new dimension to the experience.

Now many books are on tape, from classics to contemporary literature, and they are not just for the visually impaired. The library, major bookstores, and book clubs are good sources.

Families can learn and have enjoyment together as a family member reads to them. Classics, like *Swiss Family Robinson*, provide ongoing entertainment as the book is read day by day. Even young children love to hear the stories. Of course, the young child can only comprehend a portion of the content, but they are certainly richer for the experience and the time spent with their family. You can also encourage your children to perform another activity as you read, especially creative tasks, such as making grandma a birthday card, painting, making a puzzle, or playing with a building toy. Of course, this depends on the type of book that is read. By having them listen while doing something creative, both sides of the brain are stimulated. The activity of listening occupies the more analytical left side of the brain and allows the right side more free reign. The results can be quite amazing.

The following pages present ideas about how you can stretch and exercise your brain. Use the exercise ideas repeatedly, just add a little variation to them. As you exercise your brain either through the examples given here or as you develop your own exercises, remember, making up the game is as good for you as the game itself. It expands your right brain's creative capabilities. Another thing to remember is that these exercises should be fun. Let your mind play a little. This is good for the right brain, and it also ensures that you will do it tomorrow. Do them throughout the day, at the stoplight, in the shower, etc. Don't try to schedule an hour of brain exercises because, truthfully, very few people would succeed using that approach.

Children want instant success, as do adults. Be patient. Start at a successful level and then stretch a little further. Just as you do not overstimulate or extend your muscles, you let them naturally warm up, treat your brain the same way. As you attempt some of the following exercises, remember that you are going to hit a brick wall sometimes, and that's okay. Edison tried thousands of filaments before finding the right one for the lightbulb.

Brain Exercises

Add or Drop a Letter: Start with a word and add, drop, or change a letter each time, trying to return to the word or choose an ending word. Keep it unstructured and playful. Make the rule and then live by it. For example:

pop top ton tan Stan stand sand sank rank tank
thank hank hand hard harm farm form fork
pork park part past pass lass loss lops pops pop

Mental Imaging Exercise: Imagine driving to work, the grocery store, school, or anywhere you have traveled many times and preferably somewhere you will go again. Picture each thing you see in sequence as you go to your chosen place. Remember as many details as you can. The next time you actually go there, note how much you remembered and how much you missed. Try to remember all the details you missed last time. Then, when you have time to relax, remember the trip and all the new things you noticed. This will strengthen your memory and other mental facilities as you visualize the trip.

Memory and Arrangement, the Pyramid Exercise: Make a pyramid using a root word or part of a word prefix, suffix, etc., and add a letter on each time. For example:

hands

handle (handed)

handbag (handout handing handful)

handsome (handling handrail handball)

handiwork

handedness

Then try building a pyramid from these words:

jump, on, help, may, her, in, open, son, and play

First, try it without any hyphenated words. Then allow them, too. Try it with these words or your own. This will help you with Scrabble®, if nothing else.

Memorize Critical Information: Memorize information important to you; this not only stimulates your brain, but it is also useful:

Adults can memorize Pi = 3.14159265+, your drivers' license number, license plate number, dates, the first 10 prime numbers, decimal equivalents, etc. Children can memorize state capitals, multiplication tables (necessary), major decimal equivalents, major holidays, phone numbers, their address, and more. Elementary children can be taught to sing their multiplication tables to a familiar tune, which helps establish the facts in their memory. Make up a song or use one you know, like "Old McDonald" or "Three Blind Mice." Making up a song exercises the creative right brain as well as the analytical left brain.

Aural Conceptualization and Memory: Try to recreate familiar sounds mentally, with as much sound clarity as you can get. Try these: a fog horn or tugboat's long low whistle, thunder, a drill, a blender, pennies falling on cement, a motorcycle, etc. Remember Beethoven was deaf, yet he was able to hear mentally.

Sensory stimulation, conceptualization, and memory are handled by different areas of the brain. This exercise and most of the other exercises tax multiple areas of the brain. Imagining any sensory stimulus—the feel of fur or warm sun, smelling the ocean, tasting pizza, seeing fireworks, and so on—is great mental exercise.

Creative Play—Making up Spoonerisms: Take the mime to boosen up a lit and try seeing billy. (Make the time to loosen up a bit and try being silly.) Spoonerisms are usually unintentional mistakes in speech, where the first letters of two words are exchanged for each other. For example: "I fented my dender," for "I dented my fender!" Exercise your creativity and make some up.

Freeing Right-Brain Creativity: Draw as you recite poems or nursery rhymes. Doing this keeps the left brain busy with its business and allows the right brain to freely express itself.

Crossword Puzzle Creativity: Make a crossword puzzle as tight as possible. Graph paper works well for this exercise. Start horizontally or vertically with your name and include as many names of family members and relations as you can. Other words are okay, too. It is okay to use spaces for double words. Then try tools, foods, plants, cities, movies, cars, musical instruments, professions, and so on. See the example on the next page:

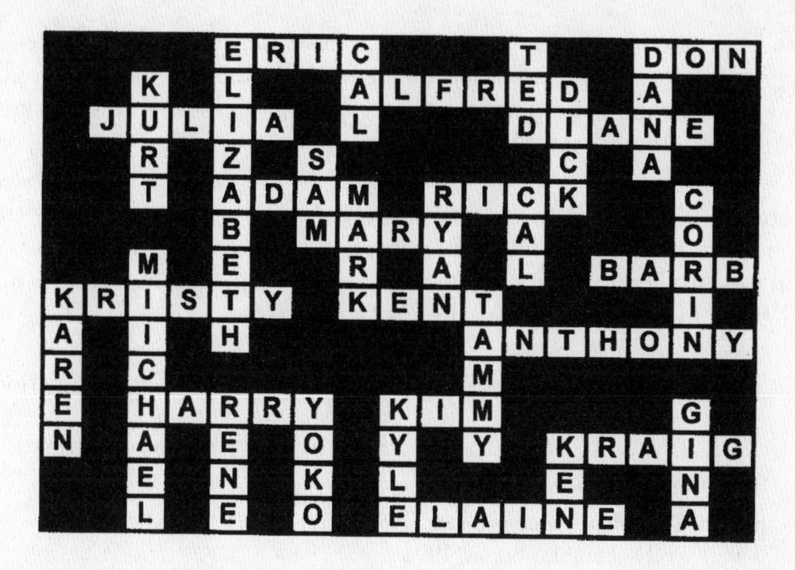

Freeing Right-Brain Thought Processes: Do you have writer's block or want to get motivated? You have 5 minutes to write everything you know or think about your subject. Don't worry about grammar, spelling, or punctuation—just write.

You can learn to allow the right-brained creative functions to flow freely, unrestricted by the left brain's need to have all things neatly arranged before any action is taken.

Remember that these exercises are only ideas to use as a springboard. The exercises in this section stimulate the less exercised right-brain functions. Right-brain exercises are not as available or perhaps not as obviously labeled "right-brained exercises" as are IQ exercises (left-brain exercises). Look for right-brain challenges covering mechanics, spatial, visual-spatial, intuition, overview, art and music, physical coordination, rhythm and dance, etc.

Libraries and bookstores carry crossword puzzles, hidden word puzzles, and challenges, like making other words from the letters of a word. You can make picture puzzles. You can make up new lines for old jokes—by substituting the original gagline with your own. See how many new ones you can generate.

Certainly, taking a class or learning art, music, dance, juggling, flower arranging, woodworking, and other hobbies are all excellent sources of right-brain and left-brain stimulation. Any new thing you learn will be a great stimulation to both hemispheres of the brain.

There are also places to get the more general IQ type questions that cover more of the left-brain functions. They are great to mix into your exercises, especially if you tend to be right-brain dominant. You may find them in the library or in the major bookstores.

Here are a few books that challenge multiple areas of the brain functions:

7 Kinds of Smart: Identifying and Developing Your Many Intelligences, Thomas Armstrong, Plume Book, 1993.

Smart for Life: How to Improve Your Brain Power at Any Age, Michael D. Chafetz, Ph.D., Penguin Books, 1992.

How to Boost Your IQ, John Bremner, Ward Lock Book, 1995.

Drawing on the Right Side of the Brain, Betty Edwards, Tarcher Putnam Book, 1989.

Computers and IQ

In the last ten years, a widespread use of personal computers and electronics has added to the media-rich environments of the industrialized nations. This may be a major reason that within the industrialized nations, overall IQ scores are rising. Computers require the most scattered thinkers to tighten up their thought processes.

We have developed a society that is more aware of logic since the extensive use of commercial and personal computers. They force us to consider our thought processes as we create practical tools that match how we think and work. We must consider the logical processes we use to arrive at a good solution.

The use of computers challenges all ages from toddlers to seniors. The young often gain knowledge through games and casual roving on the Internet. Without realizing it, their minds are being expanded and exercised. Like the 5-year-old boy who plays a computer game that directly uses and teaches logic—he just thinks it's fun! The game has an apartment building where the player has to determine which little creature goes into which apartment. A typical question goes something like this, "All the purple creatures live on the third floor, but only striped creatures live on the left-side apartments on each floor. Put the creatures in the correct apartment."

The logic involved is not unlike the logic used in the IQ test. It is similar to questions like all Bobers are Breedlins but not all Breedlins are Woolies. They both use categorization, Boolean logic, and set theory. Boolean logic and set theory are logical concepts found everywhere in our world, from computers to electrical circuits. Some call it Boolean Algebra; some call it set theory. They are all generally the same. They have become general terms for logical concepts using "*AND*," "*OR*," "*AND NOT*" (*NAND*), and "*OR NOT*" (*NOR*) to express relationships.

Each person must proceed in a logical progression. Voice mail and PBX phone systems require us to traverse through menus of options. "If you want account information, please enter your account number and press the pound key." We are traversing a tree of decisions with the possibility of arriving at countless conclusions, one decision at a time. "Checking or Savings?" "Deposit or Withdrawal?" Through *IF, THEN, ELSE* logic, we assimilate the process as we are exposed to the computer's procedural logic. "*IF* you want scheduling information, *THEN* press three. *IF* you want to make a reservation, *THEN* press four. For all other inquiries (*ELSE*), please stay on the line." These logical progressions become natural after multiple encounters with the same thought processes. The situation only becomes a variant of the same procedure.

Anyone who has attempted to do a search on the Internet has had to use his or her logical facilities in the search. With most search engines or databases, any search requires you to use logic to include the relative items and exclude the irrelevant items. For instance, to find a recent occurrence on intelligence, Boolean logic comes into play very quickly. One must search for: Intelligence *AND* Psychology *AND NOT* "Central Intelligence Agency" *AND NOT* military.

The Internet has an effect on our IQ and our ability to think. It is like an extension of our senses, an additional perception of our environment, from local to remote areas of the world. Instantly, we can contact those with similar interests. The ideas presented can be mind expanding. There is a great "think tank" available that can stimulate and stretch our mental faculties to new heights.

part 3

Giftedness, Aptitude, and Intelligence

Creativity

While not everyone possesses the creative talent of Beethoven, da Vinci, Einstein, or Edison, all human beings possess creativity. It is one of our personal characteristics and abilities. It is part of our composite character.

Until recently, people saw creativity only as part of professions unique to the arts, music, and drama. Creativity exists in all areas of human endeavor, including academia, technical professions, and politics. A creative person is anyone who brings innovation and breathes new life into any field of human activity. There are many examples: the scientist who develops a new vaccine, the coach who devises an innovative offensive tactic, the businessperson who creates a new and needed service, and the researcher who develops a new theory about human behavior. All such activities are creative endeavors in areas outside the visual and performing arts.

Creativity requires individuality, independence of thought and action, spontaneity, originality, and flexibility of action, combined with dedication to purpose and more. This type of thinking can only occur where there is a free and unencumbered flow of ideas, images, and emotions.

Creativity and originality result from mental activity peculiar to right-brain processing. Left-brain functions are sequentially ordered, analytical, logical, and temporal, while right-brain thinking is intuitive, diffuse, and spatial. The left-brain process allows the carefully ordered building of a whole from its many parts. The right-brain process allows an almost intuitive grasping of the whole in relationship to its parts.

All humans have the ability to create or to be creative. For many, this innate creative ability is squelched before they even enter school.

There is a cultural-social emphasis upon conformity, acceptance, doing the "right" thing, finding the "right" answer in the "right" way. Some can recapture the creative ability later, even in adulthood. Unfortunately, the chances are slim for later development of full potential once the person learns to suppress the individual personality and mental playfulness of the creative process.

There are tests for measuring creativity, but they do not generate results that are as mathematically specific as they are with intelligence tests. Creative talent levels cannot be broken down into specific levels of performance or potential. There are no "best" or "right" answers for creativity tests. They attempt to test divergent thinking styles. Among the types of questions used on such tests are the following:

The Untitled Story: An individual must suggest several titles for a one-paragraph story. It is scored based on: (a) quantity—the number of titles offered; and (b) quality—the originality or uniqueness of the title suggestions. For example:

Write newspaper headlines for this story:

> Jake Rush, a local private eye, was found today crushed by a grease pit hoist in an abandoned Pittman Street garage. Jake's body was stuffed in a large plastic bag. Jake had apparently been attempting to escape since he had poked a hole in the bag. Clutched in his hand were the dusty remnants of the jewels recently stolen from the internationally renowned Groist Ltd. Diamond firm. The insurance agency of Crouch, Inc., had hired Mr. Rush to assist in the investigation and recovery of the stolen jewels. Detectives theorized that Rush tried to single-handedly apprehend the criminals in their hideaway and was over-powered from behind. The jewels were stashed in a hole in the bottom of the pit, and Rush found them just before his untimely end. There is a question as to whether Rush's estate will receive the recovery reward.

Examples of Ordinary Titles: "Private Eye Found Dead"; "Detective Crushed By Hoist"; "Jake Rush Killed by Thieves"

Examples of Creative Titles: "Rush Crushed"; "Ouch-Pouch End for Crouch P.I."; "Groist Wiped out by Hoist"; "Drastic Plastic Reward"

The Untitled Cartoon or Caricature: Scored in the same way as the untitled story.

Ordinary Captions: "Help!" "Don't just stand there!"

Creative Captions: "Just checking the weather!" "Quick call 555-3267 and ask if Buz Bombstead's life insurance is paid!" "Could I borrow your umbrella?" "But you said you wanted to hang out with me!" "Is this what hang ten means?" "No, I didn't find your contact!" "Do I look like someone who's afraid of risk in a relationship?" "Now, I have acrophobia!"

Paired Words: Pairs of words that appear to have no relationship to each other are presented. The individual is asked to name a third word that is somehow related or common to the other two. See example below.

sugar	walking	(cane)
bank	story	(teller)
eye	meow	(cat's)
day	pipe	(dream)

This type of question has obvious limitations. Suggested answers are available. If the scorer is not creative enough to recognize the validity of unnamed possibilities, the question type fails as a test of creativity and becomes a test of convergent thinking ability.

Visual Fill-In: The individual might be asked to give as many interpretations as possible of what the partly completed pictures or design might represent, be, or become. For example:

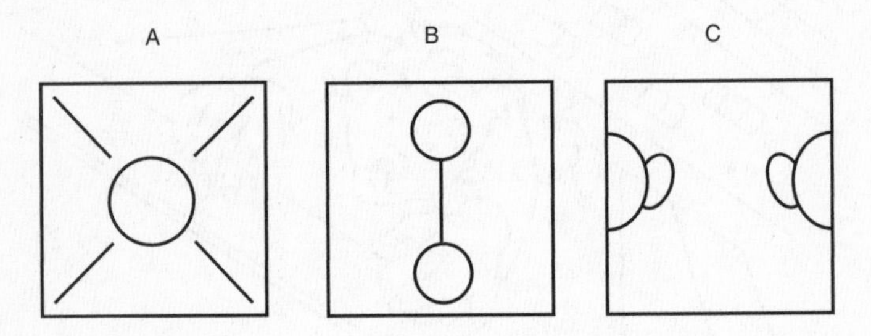

The question is scored based on quantity and uniqueness of answers.

Examples of Ordinary Answers: (a) sun; (b) barbell; (c) two cup handles

Examples of Creative Answers: (a) a four-legged spider, inside of a well, spaceship, front or rear view, a traffic circle, fat crossing guard; (b) door handle, two knotholes hooked together by a crack, stereo headset, two floating balloons, part of a necklace, old-fashioned telephone earpiece; (c) two clowns whispering, two rabbits going in opposite directions, mirror image of the left ear, mirror image of the right ear, ludicrous freeway loops

Note that the creative answers are more than unique and original; they exhibit richness and fluency of both thought and language.

Object Uses: The test taker is given an example of an ordinary object and asked to name as many different uses for that object as possible. For example, the object might be a pencil. The common answer would be to use it for writing or drawing. Creative answers might include houseplant stake, back-scratcher, string-holder, and so on.

These are a few examples of the types of questions used in creativity tests. Some of the limitations are obvious. The time required for scoring is extensive. Second, the creativity of the test designer places both upper and lower limits on the levels of creativity taken into account. Third, the creativity of the test scorer is critical. The scorer must be able to recognize the validity of relationships and possibilities that are not offered in the suggested guidelines for scoring.

There is a simpler and more effective method for determining the possibilities for creativity of an individual: the observation of the person's behavior over a period of time. One must first identify some of the behaviors that indicate creative potential and performance. Among these are independence and individuality in thought and action, along with prolific quantities of unique ideas. Another indicator is innovative production of new things. Other creative behaviors and traits include curiosity, originality, self-assertiveness, fluency, process (rather than product) orientation, self-honesty, willingness to take risks, willingness to be different, self-motivation, unusual and active imagination, ability to live with uncertainty, adaptability and flexibility, intuition, persistence, a keen and possibly unique sense of humor, sensitivity to beauty, and an awareness of emotions (one's own and those of others). Intelligence and intelligent capabilities are necessary for creativity to result in "good" products. The creative mind needs to draw on information, ideas, and concepts. IQ scores do not readily reflect the true intelligence of highly creative people. Although creative people do not necessarily have higher IQs, they would not be capable of creative endeavor as described here if their intelligence capabilities were low.

When reference is made to "highly intelligent, highly creative" persons, the reference is to individuals who are highly creative and have actual, though unregistered, IQs of 140 to 150 or more. Experience shows that a majority of unusually creative people tends to score between 120 and 139 on standard intelligence tests. Whether they are more creative than intelligent or whether they score lower on convergent types of intelligence tests because they are divergent types of thinkers is uncertain.

Gifted and Talented—More than Just IQ

Intelligence tests were originally designed to identify mentally handicapped children. Today, the focus is on gifted and talented children. A high intelligence test score is only one indicator of potential. A high IQ indicates giftedness and talent in academic and intellectual arenas. In addition, a person may be gifted in other areas. People working with children have recognized this for a long time. Some children demonstrate other abilities that are clearly outstanding. Research and studies of creativity began back in the late 1950s and early 1960s.

A person may be gifted in one or more of four areas:

- **Academic (intellectual intelligence):** The academically gifted person demonstrates outstanding potential and/or achievement in areas that require mastery of a set of formalized symbols, such as language, numbers, or both. IQ scores, achievement scores, and academic grades reflect this type of giftedness.
- **Creative:** The creatively gifted person demonstrates outstanding potential or achievement in areas that require open, original, and uniquely productive thinking or action. Creativity can be demonstrated through visual or performing arts, in academic areas, business, politics, or in the social arena. Some tests measure creativity, but these have limitations. It is particularly difficult to give them to large groups of people. A good way to identify creativity is by observing behaviors that indicate creative thinking and performance.
- **Psychomotor (physical):** The physically gifted person demonstrates outstanding potential and/or performance in activities requiring large-muscle, small-muscle, and hand-eye coordination. These include activities such as sports, dance, mechanics, and the skills required for mastering the use of fine arts media. Psychomotor abilities can be measured based on observation.

- **Social/Personal/Leadership:** The person with a gift for leadership demonstrates outstanding potential and/or performance in the areas of social and personal abilities required for leadership. Observing daily behavior is the best measurement of personality characteristics, communication abilities, and leadership skills.

IQ scores are not valid indicators of abilities in creative, psychomotor, and leadership areas. So how can you identify these gifted individuals? The best way to identify them is as stated before—to observe their behavior on a regular basis. Keep a log of the behaviors that, over time, have been singled out as reliable indicators of giftedness and talent.

In addition, there are certain behaviors exhibited by infants and preschool children that are indicators of general levels of intelligence. To identify highly intelligent children, compare their performance with average performance levels of children the same age. The following stories will give you an idea of the ways in which some gifted intelligent and creative persons have behaved as children.

Terry

Terry is now a young adult. She drank unassisted from a cup at the age of four months; cut her first teeth at five and a half months; walked at ten months; talked in simple sentences (one, two words) at ten and a half months. She dressed and undressed herself with equal ease by fourteen months and was putting puzzles together and scribbling by the age of eighteen months. She played cooperatively with other children the summer she was two. She was extremely social and competitive and was often the leader of the group.

Her outstanding physical coordination and willingness to take risks were apparent by eighteen months when she was found standing on top of the backyard swing set. Her mother told her how to get down, took her to the store, and purchased sneakers, then showed her how to climb up and down safely. She could swim well by three and a half.

Before entering kindergarten, she composed lengthy and complicated stories and free-verse poetry and could add and subtract fractions in her head. Her family highly encouraged her individuality, willingness to take risks, conceptual maneuvers, and originality. She was not taught to read, but she could write her name and numbers before entering school.

In fourth grade, Terry lead a successful student protest against writing spelling words ten times each. She and 18 other students already knew them. Terry had them all sign a petition, and she won the case by following appropriate and logical procedures.

Terry excelled academically until fifth grade, when she found it unrewarding to do all her work as fast as she could because the teacher only gave her more of the same. Terry's academic success in high school was lackluster; she graduated in the lower end of the top third of her class.

Terry was very personable. She excelled in sports, language-related subjects, and art. Her IQ was 150+, but she lost her interest in academic subjects early because she was not challenged. She developed fine art skills and played two musical instruments. Her musical performance was highly competent but not talented.

Terry grew up in a family where there was high educational attainment, but independence, individuality, and openness were prized over conformity and social acceptance, which are more likely to be valued in families of high academic achievers.

Beth

Beth reported having memories from the age of one. This is highly unusual in most individuals, even in highly sensitive and intelligent ones. She talked at an early age and could carry on a conversation with detail and fluent language by age three.

Her friends were usually older, and she was an accepted part of the adult world from a preschool age. Her powers of observation and memory were unique, and her ability to group and classify as a preschooler was evidenced by the fact that she could identify the make and model of any automobile by age four.

By four, she also could write her name, numbers, and use numerical concepts, identify forty-eight different colors, and understand the sequence of hours in the day. She took dancing lessons at age four and was extremely well coordinated, rapidly advancing to an older class. In school, she achieved extremely high marks and could read seven grades above her third-grade level.

Her achievement in other school subjects was three or more grades above level. She was a varsity athlete for four years in both high school and college and participated in every extracurricular activity available. She learned to play three musical instruments, two self-taught, and learned the rudiments of several others. She received several scholarships to college and was later offered scholarships to both law school and art school.

Beth's IQ has been measured from 130 to 145. She is both creative and intelligent and has attained high educational status and professional accomplishment as an adult. Her interest in music has continued as a hobby, and she performs with a professional group.

These persons, Terry and Beth, could easily have been identified as being intelligent and creative long before they entered school, purely on the basis of the kinds of things they did in comparison to other children of the same age. Beth's high academic achievement in comparison to Terry's is related to inner motivation, the level of personal rewards received, and the family structure in which she grew up. Beth's family allowed and encouraged independence and nonconformity in the home, but there was strong emphasis on social acceptance and conformity within the community.

Different things motivate each child. One child responds to verbal appreciation, and another desires to please those around him. Some respond to the rewards of his efforts. Others are more self motivated and, in spite of opposition or encouragement, will press on toward his desired goals. Study each child to determine what that child needs and how to encourage him or her. They need a fine balance of restriction and free reign. Each child is unique in the balance he or she needs.

Remember, creativity is important, but it is only one of the many attributes each unique individual uses to be a successful individual.

Gifted and Talented Checklist

Gifted/talented persons tend to be above average in health, coordination, and the rate of both mental and physical development. Not only do they develop more quickly in mental and physical areas, but they also exhibit greater complexity and power in specific areas of development than do those of average abilities.

Use the checklist that follows to measure yourself, another, or a child for indications of gifted and talented behavior. For each item listed, check:

1. If the behavior is never seen (1 point)
2. If the behavior is seldom seen (2 points)
3. If the behavior is occasionally seen (3 points)
4. If the behavior is seen fairly often (4 points)
5. If the behavior occurs most of the time (5 points)

I. Intellectual Intelligence

	(1) never	(2) seldom	(3) occasionally	(4) often	(5) almost always
(AS A CHILD)					
1. Chooses older playmates	___	___	___	___	___
2. Gets along well with adults	___	___	___	___	___
3. Prefers adult company to that of peers	___	___	___	___	___
4. Enjoys reading biography/ autobiography, reference books	___	___	___	___	___
(ALL AGES)					
5. Curious and inquisitive	___	___	___	___	___
6. Has large vocabulary	___	___	___	___	___
7. Uses language fluently and richly	___	___	___	___	___
8. Enjoys reading	___	___	___	___	___
9. Has abundance of ideas	___	___	___	___	___
10. Has excellent memory	___	___	___	___	___
11. Has large bank of information	___	___	___	___	___
12. Has sharp sense of time	___	___	___	___	___
13. Learns quickly and easily	___	___	___	___	___
14. Notes and uses detail	___	___	___	___	___
15. Comes up with answers quickly, easily	___	___	___	___	___
16. Answers are considered, appropriate	___	___	___	___	___
17. Quickly understands cause-effect	___	___	___	___	___

18.	Likes school—likes learning	___	___	___	___	___
19.	Understands ideas quickly, easily	___	___	___	___	___
20.	Can apply learning from one situation to another	___	___	___	___	___
21.	Finishes tasks started	___	___	___	___	___
22.	Is well organized	___	___	___	___	___
23.	Has mental and physical energy	___	___	___	___	___
24.	Is industrious	___	___	___	___	___
25.	Has strong self-motivation	___	___	___	___	___
26.	Can work independently	___	___	___	___	___
27.	Is highly competitive	___	___	___	___	___
28.	Has high personal standards	___	___	___	___	___
29.	Has strong sense of justice	___	___	___	___	___
30.	Enjoys puzzles and mental games	___	___	___	___	___
31.	Has common sense	___	___	___	___	___
32.	Has (had) high school marks (over 90)	___	___	___	___	___
33.	IQ	**below 90**	**90–109**	**110–119**	**120–129**	**130+**
		___	___	___	___	___

(If IQ is 150+, score 6 points) ___

Scores: 33–52 (low) ___

53–78 (average) ___

79–105 (bright) ___

106–132 (superior) ___

133–165 (gifted) ___

166 and over (super-gifted) ___

(See additional behaviors at end of checklist)

II. Creativity

		(1) never	(2) seldom	(3) occasionally	(4) often	(5) almost always
1.	Is flexible in thought and action	___	___	___	___	___
2.	Can live and deal with uncertainty	___	___	___	___	___
3.	Has profusion of ideas, solutions, etc.	___	___	___	___	___
4.	Ideas and solutions are unique and original	___	___	___	___	___
5.	Is personally independent	___	___	___	___	___
6.	Is uninhibited	___	___	___	___	___
7.	Is adventurous	___	___	___	___	___
8.	Is inventive	___	___	___	___	___
9.	Fantasizes, daydreams	___	___	___	___	___
10.	Has rich imagination	___	___	___	___	___
11.	Uses a lot of elaboration and detail	___	___	___	___	___
12.	Is not afraid to be different	___	___	___	___	___
13.	Takes risks	___	___	___	___	___
14.	Questions the status quo	___	___	___	___	___
15.	Offers constructive criticism	___	___	___	___	___
16.	Offers constructive alternatives	___	___	___	___	___
17.	Concerned with changing, innovating, improving	___	___	___	___	___
18.	Is sensitive to beauty	___	___	___	___	___
19.	Is sensitive to other people	___	___	___	___	___

	(1) never	(2) seldom	(3) occasionally	(4) often	(5) almost always
20. Is very self aware	___	___	___	___	___
21. Is highly self-honest	___	___	___	___	___
22. Has keen (and perhaps unusual) sense of humor	___	___	___	___	___
23. May be outgoing or may be withdrawn, but has strong self-assurance in personal projects	___	___	___	___	___
24. Emotionally stable	___	___	___	___	___
(BUT AT TIMES MAY BE)					
25. Excitable	___	___	___	___	___
26. Moody	___	___	___	___	___
27. Irritable (especially if interrupted during personal activities)	___	___	___	___	___
28. Dislikes routine and repetition	___	___	___	___	___
29. Likes to work toward goal, product	___	___	___	___	___
30. Can see the "whole" quickly	___	___	___	___	___
31. Strong sense of proportion and balance (visually, mentally, physically)	___	___	___	___	___
32. When given a choice, chooses activities requiring creative endeavor	___	___	___	___	___

Scores: 32–47 (creatively inhibited) ___

48–75 (average creativity ___

76–91 (above average creativity) ___

92–128 (superior creativity) ___

129–160 (creatively talented) ___

III. Social/Personal/Leadership

	(1) never	(2) seldom	(3) occasionally	(4) often	(5) almost always
1. Self-assertive	___	___	___	___	___
2. Bored by routine	___	___	___	___	___
3. Becomes absorbed and involved	___	___	___	___	___
4. Interested in controversial, adult, or abstract problems	___	___	___	___	___
5. Likes to organize	___	___	___	___	___
6. Extremely concerned with morals, ethics	___	___	___	___	___
7. Sets high goals	___	___	___	___	___
8. Likes and takes responsibility	___	___	___	___	___
9. Is popular, well-liked	___	___	___	___	___
10. Gets along well with others	___	___	___	___	___
11. Self-confident with all ages	___	___	___	___	___
12. Adaptable to new situations	___	___	___	___	___
13. Flexible—can change ways of getting goals without frustration	___	___	___	___	___
14. Sociable—prefers to be with others	___	___	___	___	___
15. Genuine interest in other people	___	___	___	___	___
16. Is initiator of activities	___	___	___	___	___
17. A resource for others; is naturally turned to for guidance, direction	___	___	___	___	___

	(1) never	(2) seldom	(3) occasionally	(4) often	(5) almost always
18. Is open to differences in others	___	___	___	___	___
19. Participates in many social activities	___	___	___	___	___
20. Is leader of the group	___	___	___	___	___
21. Speaks easily and fluently	___	___	___	___	___

Scores: 21–33 (definite follower) ___

34–49 (average social skills; not destined to lead) ___

50–66 (above average social leadership skills; may lead at times) ___

67–83 (superior social leadership skills) ___

84–105 (socially gifted; leadership skills) ___

IV. Physical

	(1) never	(2) seldom	(3) occasionally	(4) often	(5) almost always
1. Shows excellent general health	___	___	___	___	___
2. Shows superior physical strength	___	___	___	___	___
3. Shows superior physical agility	___	___	___	___	___
4. Shows superior physical balance	___	___	___	___	___
5. Shows superior rhythm	___	___	___	___	___
6. Is well coordinated	___	___	___	___	___
7. Is larger than average (child)	___	___	___	___	___
8. Has high energy and pep	___	___	___	___	___
9. Moves with exceptional ease and flow	___	___	___	___	___
10. Participates in sports and physical games	___	___	___	___	___

	(1) never	(2) seldom	(3) occasionally	(4) often	(5) almost always
11. Would rather participate than watch	___	___	___	___	___

Scores: 11–17 (very low physical skills)	___
18–25 (low-average physical skills)	___
26–34 (strong-average physical skills)	___
35–43 (superior physical skills)	___
44–55 (gifted in psychomotor skills)	___

Those persons who are clearly gifted and talented are often outstanding in more than one of the previous areas. Add up your scores from the previous section. Total scores for overall giftedness and talent are:

97–151 (low range of abilities)	___
152–229 (average abilities)	___
230–299 (above-average abilities)	___
300–388 (superior abilities)	___
389–485 (gifted/talented)	___
486 + (super-giftedness/talent)	___

In addition to the general behaviors listed, give an extra point for each of the following, as observed in children or in the childhood of adults.

Intellectual Intelligence

- Teaches self to read before formal instruction
- Collects things
- Organizes and maintains collection (1 point for each organized collection)
- Maintains an interest or a hobby over a long period of time
- Uses scientific approach to thinking and problem solving (analytical, methodical)

Creativity (Visual Arts)

- Likes and uses color with originality
- Chooses art projects when given a choice
- Good sense of space and design
- Is sensitive to forms and shapes
- Is sensitive to texture
- Uses a variety of lines, textures, colors, shapes in artistic creations

Creativity (Music)

- Chooses music for activity when given choice
- Can match pitch easily
- Easily remembers a melody and can reproduce accurately
- Plays toy instruments at an early age
- Invents melodies
- Invents instruments
- Reads music easily

Physical (Dance)

- Responds to music with coordinated movement of body
- Can imitate gestures and movements with ease

Summary

We have explored several things in relation your IQ: what the score means and what intelligence is and its importance. We have explored other aspects of intelligence, left-brain and right-brain facilities, computers and their relation to IQ, brain exercises, creativity, and giftedness.

Underlying all these topics are two questions: How can I get a better understanding of my intellectual strengths and weaknesses, and what can I expect and change to ensure success in my life?

Intelligence is, in its broadest sense, the ability of an individual to perceive and understand the environment and respond successfully to the problems and challenges. To be truly responsive, an individual must approach life holistically. Each strength and talent should be used, honed, and ready to work with the rest to overcome each day's challenges victoriously.

Intelligence and creativity are important attributes. However, many other attributes make up a unique individual, such as visual acuity, agility, health and emotional stability, verbal and nonverbal communication, and determination and persistence, to name a few. We must maintain a holistic view of our attributes and use them to determine our success and add to the society in new and unique ways.

The familiar term "common sense" has been around for many years. Yet it is an important personality trait. We can have the intellect of Einstein with the mental ability to calculate the speed and trajectory of a rocket, but, if we don't determine that an umbrella must be opened to keep from getting wet, we are not exercising some aspect of our abilities. Remember, even our brains take the easy route if they aren't stimulated and they aren't encouraged to learn more. If we are willing, we can learn to enjoy a greater quality of life.

In the same way, a person may have the greatest IQ and incredible analytical prowess, but without drive and motivation, a fantastic IQ score may be the only accomplishment of that person's life. In addition to IQ, common sense, motivation, creativity, and vision are important factors of personal success.

Many times, the great people of the past were inspired by those around them. We all should spend time with mentally stimulating individuals. They can help keep our brains functioning at their peak. They can challenge us to go beyond dreaming about our goals and motivate us to reach our full potential.